T0322036

Kate Hall

THE
FULL
FREEZER
METHOD

FIVE STEPS
TO TRANSFORM
HOW YOU SHOP,
COOK & LIVE

EBURY
PRESS

Ebury Press, an imprint of Ebury Publishing
20 Vauxhall Bridge Road
London SW1V 2SA

Ebury Press is part of the Penguin Random House group of companies
whose addresses can be found at global.penguinrandomhouse.com

First published by Ebury Press in 2024

www.penguin.co.uk

A CIP catalogue record for this book is available from the British Library

ISBN 9781529912180

Design: Georgie Hewitt
Illustrations: Louise Evans and shutterstock

Typeset in 10/18pt Filson Pro by Jouve (UK), Milton Keynes
Printed and bound in Great Britain by Clays Ltd, Elcograf S.p.A.

The authorised representative in the EEA is Penguin Random House
Ireland, Morrison Chambers, 32 Nassau Street, Dublin D02 YH68

Penguin Random House is committed to a sustainable future
for our business, our readers and our planet. This book is made
from Forest Stewardship Council® certified paper.

This book is dedicated to my wonderful family, and all my fellow Freezer Geeks. Thank you for supporting me and giving me the courage to share my geekery with the world.

CONTENTS

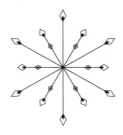

INTRODUCTION:
Your Secret Pause Button

Do you ever wish you could press a pause button on life?

I'm not talking about holidays or spa days (although they're always nice), I'm talking about having the ability to slow down some of life's pressures. I'm *particularly* referring to the relentless planning, shopping, prepping and cooking that comes with being a grown-up. It's no surprise that so many of us struggle by the time we get to dinner, and end up either:

A. Having the same old meal *again* or,

B. Ordering a takeaway while the fresh food that we bought with good intentions goes off in our fridge.

Believe me, I have been there. As a mum with two small kids, I know just how hard it is to keep that wheel spinning. It's so easy to get sucked into buying the same foods over and over on autopilot, only to suffer the crippling guilt of throwing half of it away a week later.

Wasting food wastes our time and our money, which means less of both to spend on more important parts of our lives. Not to mention, it's devastating to our planet. That's why I want to let you in on a secret. And it's so flipping simple, you're going to be amazed that you didn't already know about it.

This one simple concept has helped me and my family to almost completely eliminate infuriating food waste. It's helped us to save money, reduced our stress around daily cooking and meant we can enjoy much greater variety when it comes to our meals. And the best part is, it's highly likely that you already have access to all you need to do the same . . .

Although it won't eleviate all of life's pressures, when it comes to mealtimes, the chances are you have been *massively* underutilising your home freezer. I would bet money that when you think of frozen food, shop-bought fish fingers and peas, or maybe batch-cooked meals like soup and chilli, come to mind.

What most people don't realise is that they can freeze a huge range of food at home themselves. Now maybe you already freeze some fresh stuff, and you're thinking, *well, actually Kate, I already keep bread and milk and chillies in my freezer* (big thanks to Jamie Oliver for promoting that last one). But what about eggs, nuts, fruit and veg? What about the half jar of pesto that you didn't need for your recipe, the leftover double cream from a family gathering or even that last glass of wine that you drank, simply to avoid it going to waste?

What if all of these things could be frozen instead of going in the bin, down the sink or consumed just for the sake of it? (Although there's no judgement from me if you do finish the wine.)

By learning how to use our home freezers more effectively we can press a pause button on our food, and give ourselves the breathing space to eat it when we *actually* want it.

Having what I refer to as a 'Freezer Stash' means you always have a good selection of ingredients in stock and so there won't be any pressure to meal plan (unless you want to). And unlike batch cooking, freezing individual ingredients means that you can consume what you feel like eating, instead of forcing down whatever you decided to cook up a week ago.

Now don't get me wrong, if you love your batch cooking that's great (I myself used to be a passionate batch cook). But batch cooking is often time-consuming, and it can get pretty repetitive. Also, just because you're preparing a big quantity, it doesn't mean that you won't have a few bits and bobs left over – these often end up getting chucked into the fridge and forgotten about. The Full Freezer Method is the perfect solution to stop ingredients from going to waste. And for those who find batch cooking overwhelming, time-consuming or downright dull, my method is the ideal alternative.

In this book, I'll take you through all you need to know about The Full Freezer Method and how the process can be used in so many different ways to suit every stage of life (see The Full Freezer Loves . . . section on page 129).

Consider the money you could personally save if you stopped wasting food. Imagine being able to cook a meal from scratch without having to pop out to the shops. What if you didn't have to eat the same thing several nights in a row just to use it up, or stick to a rigid meal plan just because you already did the weekly shop? What if instead, you pressed pause on your ingredients and then knew how to quickly (and safely) defrost them, or even how to cook them from frozen? No more half-jars lost in the back of the fridge, no more bendy vegetables or fruit growing fuzz.

The Full Freezer Method is all about giving you the flexibility to reduce your food waste and save money in a way that fits into your life.

How can I be so confident that this is what you need?
Because I developed this whole concept in my own home when I was at my wits end over the food (and money) I was wasting. With a tiny baby and a toddler to care for, I desperately wanted to feel more in control of our meal times, and less like a failure because I could never make a plan and stick to it.

Truth be told, I fell in love with freezing food long before this. Just before my 21st birthday, I suffered an unexpected blood clot in my left shoulder and so my mum filled my tiny freezer with homemade meals. At that time, I had no idea of the health rollercoaster that was ahead of me (including two major surgeries to remove my top ribs), but I did very quickly get into the habit of restocking the supplies my mum had created. There was something incredibly reassuring about always having a good homemade meal to hand in case my health took a turn for the worse.

Batch cooking served me well for over a decade, but when child number two arrived I hit a wall. Even if I found the time to cook, I no longer had the motivation. The meals felt uninspiring and repetitive, and even if there was something in the freezer, we'd inevitably still opt for a takeaway.

Then one day I had a revelation. If I could freeze a meal I had cooked, surely I could freeze individual ingredients to avoid anything ever ending up in the bin. Instead of spending hours in the kitchen, I could press a pause button on a single ingredient and have it there, ready to cook, when I next had the time and inclination.

I experimented a lot with freezing, cooking from frozen and organising my Freezer Stash. I also spent endless hours trying to get my head around the food safety requirements, including getting Food Safety and Hygiene certified (Levels 2 and 3).

When the pandemic hit in 2020, I set out to share my methods with anyone who would listen. In the early days, I got a *lot* of funny looks from bemused faces, but gradually people started to take an interest. From national papers to national TV (and even a mention on *The Drew Barrymore Show!*), the last few years have been a whirlwind.

Since 2020 I have helped thousands of people to cook from scratch more easily, reduce their food waste and save money. The whole purpose of this book is to give you the confidence to do exactly that. Through these pages, I want to help you avoid the common pitfalls, shift your habits and inspire you to use your Freezer Stash; because there's really no point in freezing something if you're not going to eat it eventually! So, what do you say? Are you ready to start freezing?

Kate (aka The Freezer Geek)

What is The Full Freezer Method?

All too often we chuck food into the freezer with little thought. Bulky boxes containing only one remaining fish finger, tubs full of homemade leftovers with no labels and loose peas ricocheting around like a pinball machine each time you try to dig through a drawer. Every mealtime involving the freezer feels like an expedition into the unknown. You stand there with the door open, staring blankly, hoping that you can locate what you need. Or you just forget what you've got in there altogether, uncovering Christmas food when you go to store your summer ice lollies.

For most people, the freezer is, quite simply, where food goes to die.

This book is going to give you a complete system to overcome this.

The purpose of The Full Freezer Method* isn't just to have a well organised freezer. My method will empower you to feel more in control of your entire cooking situation. With a little kitchen management and a shift in your habits, it will help you to reduce your food waste, save money and reclaim some time.

Whether you're cooking for one, for two or for a whole family, this book is going to show you:

- How to confront your current approach to getting food on the table, and identify the changes you want to make

- How to get your current freezer food organised and cleared down

- How to freeze individual ingredients so they don't go in the bin

- How to actually use those frozen ingredients

- How to overcome the inevitable challenges you'll face along the way.

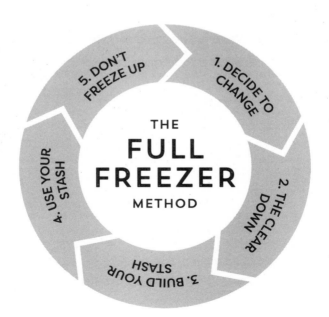

It's also going to give you the food safety knowledge and confidence that this new approach will not make you or your family sick; in fact, you may well find that your current methods are not the safest way to handle your food (see page 101).

By the end of this book, you'll have a complete picture of how you can use your freezer to make your life easier so that you're in complete control. Even when plans change or the day throws you a curve ball.

*Just a short note for those who take names literally . . . The Full Freezer Method doesn't advocate that you cram your freezer 'full' to bursting. To ensure your freezer works effectively and efficiently you should aim for it to be about 75 per cent full at all times.

Why Bother?

Changing your habits to cut your food waste might seem like a faff or more work than it's worth, so I want to share some of the reasons why you should make the effort.

Money

For starters, the average four-person household in the UK wastes £1000 per year of food that could have been eaten (£250 if you live on your own), and that's without even taking into account the extra money that is then spent replacing that uneaten food.

If you know you're guilty of binning the veggies in the fridge and opting for a takeaway instead, just think how much money you could be saving yourself and where that money would be better spent. I'm not saying you need to ditch the takeaways altogether, but making sure they're an occasional treat rather than a regular shortcut could save you some serious cash.

The Environment

If you're not overly concerned about the cash side of things, I want to throw out an appeal to your conscience instead. I'm relying here on the hope that even if you're not someone who considers themselves to be particularly 'green', you do agree that we're in the midst of a climate crisis and if there's something you can easily do, it's worth doing.

It can be difficult to make big life changes like going vegan or giving up your car. But a freezer is something that most people own already (I'm assuming you do as you bought this book!). And by simply tweaking how you use it; you can help to tackle the enormous eco-issue that is food waste.

And if you already consider yourself to be a pretty 'green' person, but you struggle with ingredients going off before you can use them, this is going to change everything for you. It's fantastic if you've decided to eat less (or no) meat, get local veg box deliveries or buy 'wonky'; but if your food is still ending up in the bin then your efforts aren't being as effective as you most likely want them to be. Freezing can help ensure your good intentions have the desired impact.

So many of us have grown up assuming that when we throw food away, it just composts and there really are no other consequences (I know that I did!). In reality, when we throw food away, we waste not just the food but all of the resources that went into producing it. All of the land, all of the water, all of the energy, as well as the carbon emissions from producing and transporting it. And of course, don't forget the packaging, which is often single-use plastic.

This is without even taking into account the sometimes back-breaking work of the producers who have put in hours of grind to get the food to us. All of it completely wasted, simply because we 'lost something in the fridge' or 'forgot that thing was in the cupboard'.

On top of these wasted resources and effort, when

food rots it releases greenhouse gases which further contribute to global warming.

Depressingly, we waste around 30 per cent of all food that is produced. What does that look like in reality? Well, in the UK, our collective annual household food waste is enough to fill the Royal Albert Hall 95 times, and that's not even including the bits you can't eat like eggshells and bones!

Our homes are responsible for the lion's share of edible food waste in the UK, with around 70 per cent of wasted food coming from domestic dwellings, rather than from shops or restaurants. I'm not telling you this to make you feel bad; the chances are you had no idea the level of food waste is so huge. I want to highlight what a huge opportunity this presents.

It can be really difficult to be greener, but reducing your food waste is something that you can tackle today. Something that can be done without any changes to government laws and regulations, without companies needing to change their packaging and without you having to spend a fortune on eco-alternatives. In fact, reducing your food waste will save *you* money, will save *you* time and will help *you* eat better.

Will tackling our collective food waste really make that much of a difference? I'll cut to the chase here . . . yes, absolutely. In fact, according to Love Food, Hate Waste, if the UK stopped wasting food for just a single day, it would do the same for the planet as taking 14,000 cars off the road for a whole year. That, to me, is mind-blowing. By shifting our perspectives on food and being less wasteful, we can have a hugely positive impact, both individually and collectively. And the more we talk about and normalise saving food instead of wasting food, the more positive actions will ripple out across the world.

Is Frozen Food Any Good?

Let's be frank. A lot of people consider frozen food to be second-rate. If I'm honest, even I have turned my nose up at the freezer aisle in the past.

What I didn't understand back then was that a lot of frozen food is simply fresh food, preserved by low temperatures. When we freeze food, we don't need preservatives like sugar or salt. The simple act of lowering its temperature stops microorganisms from multiplying and can lengthen the life of foods by months.

Whilst I would agree that some commercially frozen

foods can look less appetising (broccoli, I'm looking at you), this doesn't mean they shouldn't have a place in our kitchen (hello, broccoli soup). Commercially frozen foods can often be higher in nutritional value because freezing locks in vitamins and minerals. The nutritional value of food reduces over time, so when you consider that our so-called 'fresh' produce may have taken days to get to us, frozen food starts to look a lot more appealing!

Now of course, this isn't a book about buying pre-frozen food (although I will touch on this later), but I do want you to know that if you're worried about frozen food not being as 'good for you', you can stop worrying. Freezing is not going to make your 'fresh' food less healthy. What you should keep in mind is that if freshness is important to you, it's a good idea to buy local and freeze your fruit and veg as soon as you get it home (if you're not going to be eating it straight away).

What I don't want you to do is bin your fresh fruit or veg just because it's a couple of days old and is starting to wilt (as long as it's not mouldy). It's far better to freeze produce that you know will otherwise be binned, and build up a Freezer Stash of ingredients, so you can cook with them later. After all, a home-cooked meal made with slightly less nutritious veg is still going to be better for you than a takeaway or ready meal!

Although saving money and the environment are what I consider to be the two big motivators in adopting The Full Freezer Method, there are so many other benefits to consider too . . .

- Save time; less meal planning and food shopping

- Enjoy more variety in your meals

- Flexibility to cook single or smaller portions with no food waste

- Cater more easily for different tastes and diets

- Eat more healthily

- Stop over-eating

- Ditch your food waste guilt

- Encourage greater family involvement in mealtimes

- Expose kids to different foods

- Make it easier to teach kids (and adults!) to cook

The Full Freezer Loop

I'm introducing you to the idea of The Full Freezer Loop nice and early because understanding this is super helpful when it comes to minimising your food waste.

I find there's a lot of confusion around whether it's okay to refreeze foods, so it's helpful to be clear on the rules. Whilst it's not a good idea to refreeze food that has been fully defrosted, there is a way around this. If the defrosted food is uncooked, we can actually cook it and then freeze the cooked food. This can then be defrosted and reheated once.

The key to success is freezing cooked foods in convenient portions that are most useful to you (i.e. enough for one person, for two people, or for an entire family), rather than freezing the whole lot in one big lump. This is because food shouldn't be reheated more than once after it's been cooked, so you only want to reheat as much as you can eat immediately.

I personally love having a Freezer Stash of uncooked frozen ingredients as it means I can use them to cook a meal and, if I make too much (sometimes intentionally, sometimes accidentally), I can freeze the leftovers for another day.

This is very useful to remember not only when you

have leftovers, but also if your freezer is unintentionally switched off and you need to cook the food inside to save it. By fully understanding The Full Freezer Loop, you can save so much and never again waste delicious food because you're just not sure.

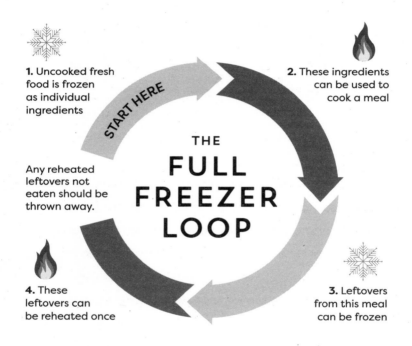

1. Uncooked fresh food is frozen as individual ingredients

START HERE

2. These ingredients can be used to cook a meal

THE **FULL FREEZER LOOP**

Any reheated leftovers not eaten should be thrown away.

4. These leftovers can be reheated once

3. Leftovers from this meal can be frozen

PHASE 1:
A Change Could Do You Good

Now, let's be frank. There is nothing particularly difficult to understand in this book. The concepts are pretty straightforward, the food safety is simple (once you get your head around it) and it can all be implemented pretty quickly.

However, there are a lot of people who attempt to adopt The Full Freezer Method without having the full picture. They dive in midway having picked up a few tips from my social media but then hit a roadblock and fall back into their old habits. I want to create lasting change. So, what I need you to do, as you read this book, is to open your mind to the possibilities and to try and fight the urge to cling to your old habits. It's going to take a bit of work initially to get yourself organised, and you need to be dedicated to the idea of changing the way that you tackle your meal planning, shopping, food prep and cooking.

Be kind to yourself while you're getting to grips with this new approach, because although the steps are simple, you'll most likely be working against decades of routine. It might take time to shift these habits, and you'll probably find that you have some freezer fails along the way, but the most important thing is that you don't give up and that you celebrate each win. Every item of food saved from the bin is a success and every meal cooked using your Freezer Stash should be savoured!

Let's begin by looking at how you shop and cook currently, then identify your pain points when it comes to getting food on the table. What is it that stresses you out the most? What is it that you really would love to change? By identifying these pain points now, you can keep them in mind as you read the rest of this book, so you'll quickly be able to identify and implement the most valuable changes.

Also, by having a clear view of how using The Full Freezer Method can improve your life, you'll be much more motivated to do the work to ditch your old habits and establish a whole new approach to cooking.

What Do You Want to Change?

What could you do differently to make life easier?
Planning, shopping, prepping, cooking . . .
or all of the above?

Use the following prompts to guide your thoughts around your current approach to getting food on the table. While you do this, remember that there is no 'right' or 'wrong' approach, only what *is* and what *isn't* working for you.

Ask yourself what is working (and can stay the same), what stresses you out and what makes you dread mealtimes?

Don't worry about solutions at this stage, as the whole point of this book is to introduce you to a new way of doing things that you're unlikely to have ever considered before. This is simply the first step towards finding your new normal.

MEAL PLANNING

What's your current approach to planning meals? (Do you plan every meal for the week ahead, plan a few meals at a time, always eat the same meals each week so don't need to plan, or plan nothing in advance?)

....

....

....

....

....

Do you feel like this is working well for you?

....

....

....

....

....

....

....

SHOPPING

What's your current approach to shopping for food? (Do you do a regular shop, do you do 'top up' shops, do you shop in-store or online, do you make a list and stick to it, or do you buy things you don't really need?)

....

....

....

....

....

....

Do you feel like this is working well for you?

....

....

....

....

....

....

PREPPING & COOKING

What's your current approach to prepping and cooking your food? (Do you cook from scratch, meal-prep, batch cook, use pre-prepped options, use ready meals, or order takeaways?)

....

....

....

....

Do you feel like this is working well for you?

....

....

....

....

....

....

....

....

You should hopefully now have a sense of what it is about getting food on the table that stresses you out, and what you're quite content with. Keep this in mind as you read on, and commit yourself to using what you're about to learn to rid yourself of the stresses.

Do You Have a Food Waste Problem?

Clearly, as you're reading this book, you want to learn how to use your freezer more effectively. There are many benefits to doing this, but I recognise that your main motivation might not be specifically to reduce your food waste (a cause close to my heart). It's quite possible that, while you don't think of yourself as having a food waste problem, you're actually throwing away a lot more than you realise.

Facing up to this reality can be a really effective way of kick-starting you into action – it might feel uncomfortable, but it gives you a solid foundation to work from. The point of this isn't to make you feel guilty or ashamed. I want to help you see what needs to change and support you on your journey (so please be as honest with yourself as possible).

SO HOW CAN YOU FIGURE OUT WHAT YOU'RE WASTING?

Take a look in your fridge and cupboards, then scan through your shopping list (if you have a regular one). Jot down any foods that you know you often or occasionally waste; it might be part-used jars, veggies that go off too quickly or maybe packaged foods that always seem to sneak past their use-by dates before you can eat them.

You could also flick through the What the Heck Can You Freeze Anyway? section to see if anything jumps out at you (see pages 197–300).

Once you have your list of frequently or occasionally wasted foods, consider which areas you feel most motivated by. What changes would save you the most money? What foods would make life easier for you by having them in stock in the freezer?

These are the foods you're going to start with once you've digested (pun intended!) the next four phases . . . Don't be tempted to go rogue and start freezing without reading on though, I promise there's a lot of super-useful advice in the coming pages!

PHASE 2:
The Clear Down

Tackling Your Frozen Wasteland (The 5C Freezer Clear Down)

It is possible to implement The Full Freezer Method gradually (steadily using up old food and freezing new stuff), but there's something incredibly satisfying about getting organised, clearing down and starting with a clean slate.

The following steps are what I recommend so that you don't begin this job and then give up part way through because you got bored or were totally overwhelmed.

It's up to you whether you work through these steps in one hit or over a few days. However, if you decide to spread the activity out, commit to completing all the steps within three or four days, otherwise you're likely to lose momentum and you'll have to start all over again.

Before you begin, make sure you've got some freezer bags in various sizes and a permanent marker. (At the time of writing, I am using Ikea ISTAD resealable bags, which I wash and reuse, and a black Sharpie pen.) Do not be tempted to use thin sandwich bags as these will not protect your food properly from the cold air. If you have any cool bags and ice packs these will be very useful too, especially if your freezer is crammed full.

SO, WHAT DO YOU NEED TO DO?

Step One: Clear Out

This step focuses on clearing out the foods that you know you'll never eat, along with any unnecessary packaging and other foods that are too freezer burnt to save (see pages 56–7). It's just a quick sweep through each drawer or shelf – we're not organising at this stage, only clearing.

The key thing here is that we don't want your freezer door to be open for too long, or your frozen food out of the freezer for longer than necessary.

Tackle one drawer or shelf at a time, emptying out the contents into your cool bag. As you empty, identify any items that are taking up space without adding any value. For example, are you storing ice packs that you rarely use? Could these live somewhere else while you're not using them? I keep ours in our picnic bag and have a few small ones in the fridge door which I pop in the freezer as and when I need them for the kids' lunchboxes.

If you have a massive bag of ice, ask yourself if you're actually going to use it. Storing ice is an awful use of freezer space, plus there are far better ways to cool your drinks (more on that later).

Identify any foods that you know you will never eat. It's important to be realistic. If the food is perfectly edible but something you just don't like, offer it to others. But if that's not an option for you, I hereby give you permission to chuck away those foods you know do not have a future with you or anyone else. You'll more than make up for the waste with your new 'Full Freezer' life. It's better to clear it out now and ensure you put your freezer to best use going forward!

The easiest options for rehousing frozen foods are obviously friends and family, but you could also look at an app like Olio to rehome your food locally.

TOP TIP

If you have a chest freezer, you could sort the contents into bags or boxes and look through each of these one at a time. The strong-handled, long-life supermarket bags are a great temporary solution to organising chest freezers, especially if yours is currently higgledy-piggledy.

Tackle your packaging

One of the reasons it is so hard to find food in your freezer is because there is no uniformity to the packaging. You might have some batch cooked meals in containers of all shapes and sizes, or shop-bought food in bags and boxes.

Standardising the way that you store your frozen food (as much as possible) is strangely satisfying, and by doing this you can create a sort of 'filing cabinet' of food. This might take a while the first time you do it but will get much quicker going forward. Believe me, this step is a game changer, so it's well worth the effort.

Grab your freezer bags and marker pen. Label each bag across the top (this is important) with whatever the food is and the best before date given on the original packaging, then pop the food into the bag. Think about the bag sizes as you do this – try to keep the bag sizes consistent for similar foods. For example, I usually put all of my bulky veggies such as broccoli or cauliflower in 2.5 litre freezer bags. Similar ingredients in the same size bags can be more easily grouped and stacked together in Step Three: Categorise.

Before you throw away the original packaging, cut off the cooking instructions (and any other info you might need, such as ingredients and allergens). You can either tape these to the outside of the freezer bag or give them a good wash and then place them inside the bag. Squeeze the air out, seal and return the bags to the freezer quickly. Do not worry about organising your food at this stage, just pop everything back where it was. Systematically tackle each drawer, shelf, bag or box.

If you have any loose items such as lollies or ice creams, group these together in freezer bags so you can clearly see what you've got.

IMPORTANT: FREEZER BURN

If you're unsure whether a particular food is okay to eat because it has freezer burn (see pages 56–7 for a proper explanation of what this is), you should know that this is not dangerous and it won't make you sick. It will impact the quality of the food though, so you may want to cut any freezer burn off foods such as meat and use any frost-bitten veggies in dishes such as curries, soups or stews where their quality won't matter as much as if they were served as a side dish.

Step Two: Capture

Once you have cleared out those unloved foods and excess packaging, the next step is to capture your contents.

Again, you need to resist the urge to organise at this stage. All we want to do here is take a *very* quick inventory of what's in your freezer. If you want to, you can do this with a notepad and pen or a spreadsheet, but I find it's far quicker to grab my phone and take an individual snap of each bag of food in the freezer (see sample images below).

By taking photos, not only can you capture what you've got in stock very easily, but you can also *see* exactly how much of each food you've got available. This will be super helpful in Step Five: Consume.

Simply work through one drawer, shelf, bag or box at a time, returning the food immediately to your freezer. Once you've snapped a photo of each food item you can move on to Step Three: Categorise.

Step Three: Categorise

Once you have captured what you've got in stock and your food is all back in the freezer, it's time to figure out your categories.

Now, it may well be that you already know what these are off the top of your head. If not, grab a cuppa and take a few minutes to scroll through the pictures you've just taken, sorting them into groups of similar items. To give you an idea of what these might be, my freezer is split (from top to bottom) into:

- **Baked goods**

- **Fruit**

- **Cooked meats and leftovers**

- **Dairy**

- **Veggies**

- **Pantry items (leftovers I've frozen that started out in the cupboard)**

- **Fish and seafood**

- **Raw meat**

IMPORTANT: RAW MEAT & FISH

Raw meat and fish should always be kept at the bottom of your freezer and away from other foods to reduce the risk of cross-contamination. If you don't currently have the space to store meat in your bottom drawer, you'll find the tips on pages 204–7 helpful. If you do have to put raw meat alongside other foods in your freezer, ensure they are foods that will be cooked before eating such as vegetables. And if your freezer ever defrosts with raw meat in any of the upper drawers, be sure to dispose of any foods below as these may have become contaminated.

Once you have these categories in mind, it can be helpful to sort the photos on your phone into albums so that you can easily see what's in each category (see www.thefullfreezer.com/freezerinventory for how to do this). You can, of course, complete this process with just a piece of paper and a pen, if preferred.

This step makes it so much easier to see exactly what's in your freezer. It will also help you with the next two steps; rearranging your freezer and then planning how you're going to use what you've got!

Step Four: Contain

Now, this is where the magic happens! Take another look at your photos organised into their categories and think about how much space you'll need for each category.

Depending on your freezer space, you might be able to allocate a whole drawer or shelf to each category, or it might be that you need to carve up your drawers to squeeze two or more categories in each one.

Before you move anything, look around the house for any containers that can help you divide up the space that you have. These could be shoe boxes or plastic storage containers, or even ice cream tubs and fruit punnets.

If you don't have anything that fits your needs, don't worry. You can still reorganise your foods without any containers, plus it's likely that your categories will change anyway as you read this book. These are just useful ways to divide up the freezer space and avoid items drifting.

You may also want to make temporary tags or labels for each drawer, shelf, bag or box, or to colour-code each section (e.g. red for meat, blue for fish, green for veggies).

On page 64 I run through further storage and labelling options that you can use once you've developed your categories to fit your needs, but at this stage I really encourage you simply to use what you've got.

Empty out one drawer into your cool bag or box, then quickly rearrange the foods for that drawer's new category. Grab the next drawer and do the same, quickly rearranging your food into its new home. Place the freezer bags so that they're standing up, with the labelling at the top of each bag visible. This will allow you to flick through your Freezer Stash more easily. It will also mean that if you don't have a designated 'open-freezing' space, you should be able to slide a tray into the top of your drawers (see page 72).

Repeat until your Freezer Stash is neatly arranged by category and your frozen food wasteland is a distant memory.

Step Five: Consume

Now that your freezer is well organised, containing only foods you actually want to eat, it's time to plan to use up those stocks and clear the decks for a good defrost and clean.

The time this takes will obviously depend on how much freezer space you have, and how much food you've got squirrelled away. What I love about this step is that it's a great introduction to the feeling of achievement you get when you build a Freezer Stash.

Because you can more easily see what you've got in your freezer, it'll be easier for you to cook using its contents (no more Arctic expeditions). As you use up those stocks, you can get away with buying less over the next days or weeks, saving yourself time and money.

To get started, just focus on coming up with three meals that you can make using stuff from your freezer. It's particularly helpful to use up foods that are taking up a lot of space first, so if you've got any home-cooked meals like cottage pies or lasagne, think about putting them to good use.

You may also want to think about your plans for the next week and whether any of these meals or foods will make your life easier when you've got a busy day ahead.

If you don't have foods in your freezer that will make an actual meal, consider whether anything you've got could be used alongside fresh foods, or simply be made into a snack. If you find yourself with a random selection of foods that you really do not want to use, circle back to Step One and ask yourself honestly if you're ever going to want to eat them. If not, it's better to rehome or bin them now.

Now jot down your three meals (or snacks) on a piece of paper, stick it up on your fridge and commit to eating them all within the next week. Then the same time next week you can come up with another three meals until you've managed to clear your entire current stock of food.

If you want to clear down your freezer faster, of course you can plan more meals, but I find having some flexibility makes it a bit easier to ensure you eat what you've planned at some point throughout the week. If you're desperate to clear down what you've got as quickly as possible, you could always plan a freezer clear-down party with family and friends and serve them up some freezer tapas (aka whatever random stuff is in your freezer!).

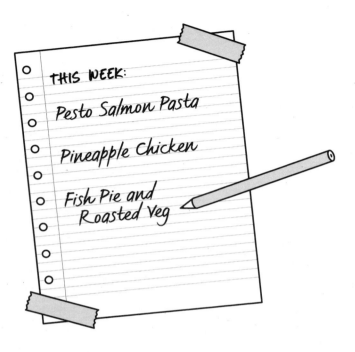

It isn't necessary to totally empty your freezer before you defrost it, or before you start to implement The Full Freezer Method, but it really does help to give yourself some space to work with and to ensure any new foods you buy are frozen using the techniques in this book (see pages 68–85). That way you can start making better use of the space that you have got as soon as possible!

Defrost Like a Boss

Can I tell you a secret? I really love defrosting freezers.
I know . . . it's a bit weird, but there's something incredibly
satisfying about getting all of that ice cleared out and
reclaiming the space.

I have a super-simple hack that makes it really easy
to do (so much so, you might even enjoy defrosting your
freezer too!). I use bowls of hot water to melt the ice (see
page 46) which reduces the need to hack and scrape.

TOP TIP

Defrost chest freezers at least every
12 months and tall freezers every 6 months, or
whenever the ice build-up is more than half a
centimetre thick.

If you have a frost-free freezer, you can of course skip this defrosting step, but it's still a good idea to give your freezer a clean at least once or twice a year. If you skipped over The 5C Freezer Clear Down (page 27), this is your sign to go back and take action!

DO I REALLY *HAVE* TO?

I know it's probably a job you've been putting off. You might well currently have to endure that horrible scraping sound just to get your iced-up freezer drawers in and out. I've even seen drawers frozen shut, with the contents abandoned, like a sacrifice to the freezer gods.

When your freezer gets overly frosty, it has to work harder, which makes it more expensive to run. You also can't store as much in it, and believe me, once you realise how much you could be freezing, you're going to want as much space as possible.

If this sounds familiar, it's time to take a deep breath and face the fact that your freezer is not going to defrost itself.

You. Have. Got. This.

OKAY, OKAY . . . SO, WHAT DO I NEED?

There are a few things that are helpful to have to hand before you get started:

- ☑ **Cool bags or plastic/cardboard boxes**

- ☑ **Newspaper** (useful for insulating foods; if you don't have any, just make sure you pack your foods closely together)

- ☑ **Ice packs** (frozen)

- ☑ **Old towels, heavy blankets or wool-insulated packaging**

- ☑ **Bowls/pans that fit in your freezer**

- ☑ **Oven gloves** (depending on the bowls/pans you're using)

- ☑ **Freezer trays (see page 62) or deep baking trays**

- ☑ **Rubber gloves**

- ☑ **Plastic or wooden spatula or ice scraper**

- ☑ **Dustpan and brush**

- ☑ **Freezer thermometer** (optional – ideally wireless with remote sensors, see page 60)

BUT I'VE STILL GOT FROZEN FOOD . . .

The chances are there's never going to be a great time to defrost your freezer. The good news is that it's possible to keep your frozen food safe while you defrost:

1. If you have ice packs, freeze these before you start so you can pack them amongst your food.

2. Wrap any frozen foods in newspaper (if you have some) and pack it tightly into cool bags, or into plastic or cardboard boxes, along with the ice packs.

3. Cover the bags or boxes with thick towels, heavy blankets or wool-insulated packaging.

4. Put the bags or boxes somewhere cold; if you have space, this could be your fridge turned to its lowest setting. Otherwise a garage, balcony or patio should be suitable, although if it's outside make sure your food is well protected from any pests.

5. Immediately crack on with defrosting your freezer (see pages 46–8). Once you're done, your food can be returned to the freezer as long as the food still has ice crystals in it. If it doesn't, any raw foods can be cooked and refrozen (see pX).

4 steps to
defrost like
a boss

1. Towels down & freezer off

2. Hot water bowls

3. Scrape (no knives)

4. Wipe & dry

Repeat
2 & 3 until
clean

Let's get defrosting!

1. Lay dry towels (not your best ones) across the bottom of the cabinet, and if you have a tall freezer, place them on the floor as well (save one towel to pop in the doorway when you get to step 4). Switch your freezer off and remove the drawers or baskets. If you have a chest freezer, there may be a drain at the bottom to release any excess water; leave this area clear so that you can drain the water from here as needed.

2. Carefully place half-filled bowls or pans of hot (but not boiling) water inside your freezer. Remember you might need to use oven gloves to protect your hands. Close the door and leave for 15 minutes.

3. While the hot water is working its magic, give your drawers a quick wash in hot soapy water and dry them off. Some drawers have removable fronts so that you can more easily wash out any crumbs.

4. After 15 minutes, take the bowls out of the freezer and pop your last towel down in the doorway of the freezer. Put on some rubber gloves and remove as much frost and ice as possible using a plastic or wooden spatula or ice scraper. Remove large pieces of ice by hand and use a dustpan to scoop up any small pieces. Empty them

TOP TIP

If possible, pop a freezing tray (see page 62) or a deep baking tray on top of the towel in the bottom of the freezer to collect as much ice and water as possible.

straight into your sink. If there's still a lot of ice, remove the towel from the doorway so you can shut it and repeat the hot water bowls as many times as necessary.

Never ever be tempted to use anything sharp to scrape off the ice as you could puncture your freezer!

5. Once you've cleared out all of the ice, remove the towels and pop them straight into the washing machine. Wipe the inside of the freezer with warm water (not too much) and dry thoroughly with a clean towel or cloth. Don't forget to wipe down the inside of the door and the seal around the door too (a chopstick wrapped in a microfibre cloth is a good way to really dig into the crevices of your door seal).

If your freezer has any stubborn dirt or stains, use warm water with bicarbonate of soda or vinegar (1 litre of warm water with 2 tablespoons of bicarb or equal parts warm water and vinegar) rather than shop-bought cleaning products, as these may release harmful substances or odours.

6. Return any drawers or shelves to the freezer, then allow the whole freezer to airdry for 10–15 minutes. Put your thermometer sensors into the freezer (if using), close the door and switch the freezer back on. If you have a fast-freeze setting, use this to speed up the cooling process.

IMPORTANT: DON'T RISK IT

You might have seen certain hacks to speed up defrosting your freezer by using a hairdryer or heater. PLEASE DO NOT DO THIS. Mixing electricity and water is potentially lethal, even if you aim to be careful.

RESTOCK & RELAX

Once your freezer is colder than wherever you're storing your food, you can start to restock it; the time it takes will vary from model to model. If you don't have any food in stock when you defrost, it's best to let your freezer drop down to -18°C before buying any new frozen food or freezing any fresh food.

Once it reaches a temperature of -18°C, don't forget to turn off the fast-freeze setting (if you used it); leaving this on could damage your freezer!

If you don't have a freezer thermometer, just leave your freezer for at least an hour or two before you move your food back into it, and leave it 24 hours before buying any new frozen food or freezing from fresh.

A quick word on insurance

I cover this in more detail on page 176 (what to do in a freezer-related emergency), but before you start building your Freezer Stash, I want to flag that it's possible to cover the contents of your freezer in your home contents insurance policy. There will usually be a limit on the age of the appliance, and you may not be covered in some scenarios, but it's worth knowing where you stand before you load your freezer up with food!

WHAT NEXT?

You should now be clear on why you want to shift your habits. You should also have a well organised freezer, and you should have some insight into the foods you're actually wasting.

Now, let's move on to my favourite bit . . . let's dive into building your Freezer Stash!

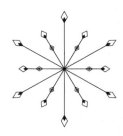

PHASE 3:
Building Your Freezer Stash

For the removal of any doubt at this stage, I want to make it clear that when I talk about having a Freezer Stash, it's not a stock of frozen meals. Remember, The Full Freezer Method is *not* about batch cooking (although it does work really well alongside batching, if that's your thing).

My Freezer Stash is best described as a filing cabinet of frozen ingredients, which is organised with ease of access in mind. Consistently sized freezer bags are clearly labelled so that everything has its place and everything you need can be found with minimal effort.

Far too often our freezers become somewhere we sling leftovers and shop-bought fodder with little thought for locating (or even identifying) the contents later. In doing this, we're simply not making good enough use of this genius bit of kit.

So, whether you already use your freezer (but know it needs some love) or you currently only house ice in there, I want to take you through the key things you need to know to build your own Freezer Stash.

TOP TIP

Label your freezer bags *before* you put the food in them, and definitely prior to putting them in the freezer. If your freezer bag does not have a wide strip across its top, it will be more difficult to write on with food inside it. And if the bag is cold and damp, writing on it will be pretty much impossible!

Start with the End in Mind

I cannot stress enough how important it is to consider how you'll use your food after freezing it. I've lost count of the number of messages I've had from people saying they find it a nightmare defrosting food in time for dinner. I've witnessed the ritual 'smashing' or 'stabbing' of the entire frozen foodberg so that the whole thing doesn't have to be defrosted. And in the past, I have myself made that inevitable call for takeaway because 'it'll just take too long' from the freezer.

All of these scenarios are avoidable with just a little bit of forward planning. Because when you prep your food before freezing with some thought about how you might like to use it, you can ensure it will defrost quickly. In some cases it could even be cooked (or eaten) straight from frozen.

For example, by butterflying chicken breasts (see page 205) and freezing them flat as individual pieces, they can be defrosted far faster than a whole pack of chicken slung into the freezer without a second thought. They'll also take up far less space, allowing you to freeze more. This goes for minced meats too. By buying the largest possible pack and separating it into smaller flat frozen portions you can save money, space and time.

In this section, I share all of my methods to minimise defrosting time and to best utilise the space that you've got. But before I do, there are five golden rules you need to bear in mind . . .

The Five Golden Rules

Rule 1. Don't Freeze It If You Won't Eat It

I know, I know. Once you realise that you *can* freeze something, it's tempting to freeze *everything* (particularly if you're trying to avoid food waste). But you should never waste freezer space on something you know you'll never actually eat.

Whether it's poor quality, or it's a meal or an ingredient that you just don't like very much, it's best not to take up valuable freezer space with something that you can't see yourself eating. It might also be the case that you simply have an excessive amount of something that you just can't envisage yourself getting through any time soon.

This doesn't mean the food should be consigned to the bin though; could you share it with someone who wants it using an app like Olio, or by dropping it off at your local food bank? Or could you give it to family, a friend or a neighbour? Setting up a WhatsApp group to share unwanted food is a great way to avoid any waste, and you might end up helping someone out without even knowing it!

Rule 2. Test For Success

You might already have a good idea of what you would like stashed away in your freezer, but before you get too carried away, remember it's always a good idea to do a test run first.

Although most foods can be frozen, you might find that not everything is to your taste after freezing, or that you prefer one approach over another (see rule 3). Instead of diving in and filling a whole drawer with the spoils of your allotment or seasonal veg box, freeze just a small amount and then use it.

Once you know that how you're freezing particular foods works for you, you can then crack on and freeze as much as you like. Doing that test first can really help to avoid a lot of potential future waste!

Rule 3. Tweak and Try Again

While some foods can only really be frozen using one practical approach, most can be frozen in a few different ways. For example, carrots may be frozen in batons or chunks (for roasting), slices (for steaming and boiling), cubes (for frying), or grated (to add to dishes such as Bolognese).

If you freeze a food in one particular way, use it and then dislike the outcome, don't assume that you can't possibly freeze that ingredient again in future. Think about whether there's another way that food can be frozen, or another way it can be used. Also, be sure to check out the cooking tips in Phase 4 of this book (see pages 115–126). Just because it didn't work out the first time, it doesn't mean you can't find an alternative that suits you better!

Rule 4. Don't Fear the Burn

Freezer burn occurs when food is poorly wrapped or has been in the freezer for longer than recommended. The food can appear white or greyish, mottled and may be covered in ice crystals. Many people on seeing this assume the food is unsafe to eat, and understandably so; it can look pretty unpleasant!

In reality, freezer burn is just dehydration. The moisture in the food has essentially been sucked out and into the cold atmosphere of the freezer, leaving the food looking like a sad version of its former self.

Eating food with freezer burn won't make you sick, but it may not taste as good or the texture might be less appealing.

To avoid freezer burn forming, wrap food tightly, squeeze the air out of any bags or wrapping being used and make sure you use proper freezer bags (not thin sandwich bags). You can also vacuum seal foods such as meat and fish to better protect them (see pages 84–5).

If you do discover freezer burn, you can just trim off the affected area. Or if the food is in small pieces and is covered in ice crystals, simply use these ingredients where the textural changes will be less noticeable, such as in a stew, pie or curry.

Rule 5. Ditch the Defrosting!

Okay, so sometimes you'll need to defrost foods before eating or cooking them, but this isn't always the case! For example, if you've 'started with the end in mind' and washed, dried and chopped or sliced your veggies before freezing them, they can be cooked straight from frozen. In fact, it's actually best to cook them straight from frozen as it allows any excess moisture to evaporate quickly instead of the food losing structure and turning soggy while defrosting.

There are also some foods that are best eaten straight from frozen. If you haven't tried frozen fruit yet, you're missing out . . . in my opinion, there's something infinitely more delicious about a frozen raspberry than a fresh one (that goes for grapes too). They turn into almost a sorbet and melt on your tongue with a far more intense flavour. And for those fretting about sensitive teeth, you could use them straight from frozen in sorbets, ice cream or smoothies instead.

You may even find you prefer the texture of some puddings or cakes while they're still frozen (you haven't lived until you've enjoyed a chocolate brownie or cheesecake straight from the freezer). Just be careful if it's a food that freezes very hard as you don't want to break your teeth!

So, as you read this book, rid yourself of the misconception that you need to defrost everything; the freezer can be far more convenient than you've been led to believe.

TOP TIP

Bananas are the perfect food to use straight from frozen. Freeze in slices, then blitz in a blender, (scraping down the sides regularly) until they form a light and fluffy soft scoop ice cream. Add other frozen fruits, peanut butter or chocolate spread to change the flavour, and serve immediately!

What Kit Do You Need?

The good news about getting started with The Full Freezer Method is that you probably own most of the things that you'll need to begin. You might decide to invest in specific 'kit' once you get into it, but there's no reason you can't get going with what you've already got.

The most important thing is that your freezer is suitable for the job. What you need to check is that it has a four-star freezer rating (see the symbol below). This means that its temperature is -18°C or colder, making it suitable for freezing both fresh and pre-cooked foods. You want a freezer that goes colder than -18°C so that you can fast-freeze your foods to help retain their quality (see page 69). If your freezer rating is less than four stars you can find out more about how to use it on page 178.

On a related note, you should make sure that your freezer is definitely cold enough before you start freezing.

Even if your freezer has an in-built display telling you the temperature, it's worth investing in a fridge/freezer thermometer, ideally with an external digital display. This is because the temperature can vary between the bottom/ top and front/back of the appliance, and you can only really get an accurate reading with the appliance door closed. Having an external display is also really useful if you have a power cut, as your food can actually remain frozen for as long as 24–48 hours providing you don't open the door.

The only other item that I strongly recommend investing in, if you do not already have one, is a food probe thermometer. These are often assumed to just be for cooking meat, but they're actually massively helpful when you're cooking from frozen or reheating meals. By using a probe thermometer, you can cook to internal temperature instead of time, allowing you to make sure your food is heated to a safe temperature without overcooking it.

I was lucky enough to be gifted a good-quality food probe thermometer when I set up The Full Freezer and I haven't looked back since; I genuinely couldn't cook without it these days! You can find the temperatures you need to be cooking to on page 106.

Checklist

Need to Have

☑ **Baking parchment** (ideally reusable)

☑ **Food probe thermometer**

☑ **Four-star rated freezer**

☑ **Freezer bags** (see page 64)

☑ **Fridge/freezer thermometer with external display**

☑ **Ice-cube tray** (ideally lidded, with a silicone base)

- ☑ **Ice packs or ice cubes**

- ☑ **Mesh pop-up tents**

- ☑ **Permanent marker pen**

- ☑ **Stackable freezer trays, or any flat surface you can fit in your freezer** (e.g. baking trays, plastic container lids, fruit punnets or picnic plates) – you may already have an open-freezing tray in your freezer, which you most likely use for ice cubes!

Probably Already Have

- ☑ **Chopping boards** (different ones for vegetables, meat, fish, cooked foods)

- ☑ **Colander, slotted spoon or tongs** (for blanching)

- ☑ **Grater**

- ☑ **Large bowl** (for blanching)

- ☑ **Large saucepan** (for blanching)

- ☑ **Sharp knife** (and ideally a knife sharpener)

- ☑ **Vegetable peeler**

Nice to Have

☑ **Bag holder**

☑ **Blanching basket**

☑ **Food processor** (including slicing/grating disk)

☑ **Measuring cups**

☑ **Stick blender**

☑ **Vacuum sealer**

☑ **Vegetable chopper**

☑ **Vinyl freezer drawer labels**

☑ **Weighing scales**

What you'll actually need to get started will depend on what you want to freeze, so don't rush out and buy lots of stuff. For the first year of The Full Freezer Method, I made do with baking trays and picnic plates, so you can definitely make things work without spending a fortune!

If you're looking to invest in some new kit or are starting from scratch, you can find most of the items listed above in my Amazon shop (www.amazon.co.uk/shop/thefullfreezer); please note these are simply the products that I use, and that work well for me.

Creating Your Freezer Filing Cabinet (Freezer Storage Solutions)

As mentioned on page 31, I use freezer bags to keep my food organised (Ikea ISTAD bags are my preferred brand at the time of writing this).

The main reason for using plastic freezer bags (*not* sandwich bags – they are far too thin!) instead of tubs, glass jars and even silicone or PEVA freezer bags is that they take up far less space, so you can fit more food in your freezer.

They're also a cost-effective way to get started, as reusable bags can often be very expensive (I've seen brands charging as much as £22 for a single bag!). That isn't to say that you shouldn't invest in reusable freezer bags, but I don't want the cost of doing so to put you off starting to freeze and save your food from the bin.

What I like about the Ikea bags is that they come in a variety of sizes and have a coloured strip across the top, which is perfect for labelling. By writing across the top of the bag (instead of on the front), it's far easier to flick through to find what you need. If you write on this strip with a permanent marker it will stay labelled in the freezer, but if you soak the bag in warm soapy water the writing will wash off (although your writing may get rubbed off particularly well-loved bags in the freezer). Bags can easily be re-labelled if necessary (just wipe the top strip dry before re-writing your label).

The stiffness of the bags ensures that they can be turned fully inside out when washed and stood up on a clean tea towel to dry out, with no need to hang them over anything. For me, this is key to making sure that I actually reuse the bags. To store them, I simply group the same-sized bags together, fold them in half and place them inside another bag of the same size. All of these 'bagged' bags then go inside one large bag and live in a kitchen drawer.

Because most of the foods I freeze are open-frozen, rather than flat-frozen (I explain what this means on pages 72–4), I find the bags last very well. Any that do split or break, I wash and then put into soft plastic recycling (there are collection points at most major supermarkets in the UK).

When you start to store your foods in freezer bags, the key is to line them up like a filing cabinet, grouping the same-sized bags together and standing them upright with the written labels all facing the same way. Because they're flexible, it's easy to fit lots of these bags in your freezer without overcrowding. Remember to squeeze the air out of the bags to minimise the space they take up and better protect the food.

You can of course use airtight tubs or glass containers if you prefer (only toughened glass; you don't want anything breakable in your freezer!) But this means that you cannot fit as much in the freezer and, as the contents of the tub run out, it will be taking up a lot of space without much benefit.

What About Compostable Freezer Bags?

When I discovered compostable freezer bags, I was
so excited. I was delighted at the prospect of ditching
the plastic-heavy storage element of The Full Freezer
Method; like most people, I think we need to reduce our
reliance on plastic wherever possible.

Although the compostable bags I found were more
expensive and couldn't be re-labelled, I thought that
at least I could use fewer plastic bags. It's worth noting
as well that compostable bags are different from
degradable freezer bags, which are still made of plastic
but contain components that make them break up into
microplastics faster.

I used compostable bags for a while (for raw meat
and fish), but I felt a bit uneasy about how best to
dispose of them. On delving into the topic, it transpired
that they aren't such a great 'solution' after all. Unless
the bag is certified as home compostable (it will have
a logo to indicate this), and you have a proper home
composter, it isn't actually possible to dispose of the bag
in a way that it will properly break down. These bags
need particular conditions (like oxygen) to compost fully.
If they go into landfill, there isn't any oxygen and so they
won't properly degrade.

What's more (at the time of writing), if compostable

bags go into industrial composting facilities, they generally end up getting fished out because there's no obvious way for those running the plant to know that they are compostable.

On the bright side, they're at least made of natural materials, but for the moment, most home-compostable freezer bags are far too thin to be effective. The better quality, industrially compostable freezer bags can't be composted at home!

I live in the hope that someone far cleverer than me will come up with a solution to overcome this.

The Secrets to Successful Freezing

Let's be honest, at some point we've all had a freezer that's half-full of almost empty boxes. Or we've frozen something in such a big portion that it's taken three days to defrost in the fridge.

By adopting the freezing methods below, we can make more efficient use of our freezers. We can better use the space that we have, defrost foods faster and ensure that we only use as much as we need. These are such simple techniques, but they will radically improve your freezer game. They're your first step into joining the slightly smug world of the Freezer Stash owner.

IMPORTANT:
FAST-FREEZE SETTING

Some freezers have a setting which allows you to temporarily lower the temperature so that you can freeze fresh or cooked foods faster. I know it's a bit boring, but it's worth digging out your instruction manual (or looking it up online) to make sure you use this setting correctly. Some manufacturers recommend that you switch the fast-freeze setting on a specific amount of time in advance. And with some models, you will need to remember to turn the setting off; for the latter, I've found setting a reminder on my phone to be the best option.

Open-Freezing (Avoiding the Foodberg)

All open-freezing means is that you freeze your food spread out on a lined tray before putting it into a bag or container. The reason for doing so is that the food freezes faster and doesn't form a clump (or foodberg, as I call it). This helps to better preserve the quality of the food, as well as allowing you to use the exact amount you need without having to hack at your food like some sort of primal hunter.

Do make sure you always line your tray, ideally with reusable baking parchment; this is stronger than the disposable stuff and is a worthwhile investment as you'll use it for freezing most items. If you try open-freezing without lining the tray, I promise you'll only do it once. It's amazing how solidly food can stick to your tray, leaving you with the frustrating situation of having to defrost the whole lot and use it all in one go.

Generally speaking, your food should only need to be left on the tray for a few hours to freeze through, but don't panic if you forget about it and end up discovering it the next day. The food will still be safe to eat (even if it's been a few days), although, from a quality perspective, it's best not to do this. You'll also find leaving food uncovered for more than a few hours in the freezer can result in the food absorbing 'freezer' smells, or if you're freezing something pungent, like onions, you're likely to find your other food picks up their pong (so it's best to always open-freeze these on their own!).

I use stackable trays which are specifically suitable for use in the freezer, but you can absolutely get started using baking trays, fruit punnets, picnic plates or even the lids of plastic containers. You just need to make sure they fit in your freezer before loading them up. If you want to freeze a few things at once, you could use deep tins of different sizes so that they can be stacked on top of each other without squashing the food, or you could place a small tin in the centre of your tray so that another tray can be balanced on top.

You may already have a flat tray in your freezer (often used for freezing ice cubes). If you have drawers in your freezer, it can be useful to remove one drawer to give you a designated open-freezing space, or you might be able to use the icebox in your fridge (just make sure it has a four-star freezer rating). Alternatively, once you've got your freezer organised, you should be able to slide a tray in on top of the food that you're storing (see page 72).

Foods that can, or should, be open-frozen before storing can be found in the 'What the Heck Can You Freeze Anyway?' section, marked 'O.F.' (see page 201).

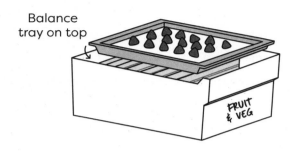

Balance tray on top

FRUIT & VEG

Once your food is frozen through, it can be moved to a labelled freezer bag. I label across the coloured strip at the top of the bag so I can flick through the tops to find what I need without having to take the bags out. Always squeeze as much air out of each bag as you can before resealing, to help protect the food inside. You can freeze in airtight containers if you prefer, but these will take up far more space and make it harder to find what you need quickly. The joy of using freezer bags is that they protect your food and their volume reduces as you eat it up.

Flat-Freezing (The Ultimate Space-Saver)

There's often confusion between open-freezing and flat-freezing because when you open-freeze, you spread your food over a flat surface. The difference is that flat-frozen foods are frozen in a bag so that they will lie flat or they can be stood upright in your freezer. This works for foods that are soft or wet in texture, such as tinned tomatoes, coconut milk, or cooked foods like soup or Bolognese.

You simply need to label your bag across the coloured strip at the top with a permanent marker pen noting what the food is, how much there is and the date frozen, then pop the bag in a cup or jug, folding the seal outwards. This helps to avoid the seal getting dirty when you pour the food in. If you prefer, you can buy bag holders, but I've never felt the need for one of these. Once your food is in the bag, seal it up, carefully squeezing the air out as you do.

Next, lie the bag flat on your lined tray and pop it in the freezer, making sure the tray is flat, then freeze until the food is solid.

It's important that when you freeze foods in this way, you freeze everything in usable portions as you'll need to use it all at once (unless it's frozen very thinly, in which case you could snap the food inside the bag and just use some of it).

The brilliant thing about flat freezing is that the food takes up far less space in the freezer and can be defrosted very quickly. You can even run the bag under your cold tap (or pop it in a dish of cold water) just long enough for the food to be released from the bag, so you can then throw it into whatever you're cooking while it's still frozen. Just make sure your dish is piping hot before serving.

If you have more than one bag of food to flat freeze, you can lie them on top of each other with a sheet of baking parchment between them to stop the bags sticking together. It's best not to layer more than three small bags or two large bags though, as this can stop them from freezing flat, and slows down the freezing process.

A list of the foods that can be flat-frozen before storing can be found in the 'What the Heck Can You Freeze Anyway?' section, marked 'F.F.' (see page 201).

Cube-Freezing (Tiny Cubes of Joy)

For wet foods that tend to be used in small quantities such as tomato purée, pesto or curry pastes, the humble ice-cube tray is your best friend. For larger cubes, you could use baby weaning cube trays or silicone moulds. Before you use your favourite ice cube tray though, it's important to know that anything with a strong smell or colouring can stain and taint the plastic.

Once your food is frozen, the cubes can be transferred to a freezer bag, ready to use when you need them.

Before freezing your foods, you may like to check how much your ice-cube tray holds. This can be accurately gauged/measured by freezing ice cubes and then allowing them to melt in a jug. Once they've melted, divide the total amount of liquid by the number of cubes in the tray.

A list of foods that can be cube-frozen can be found in the 'What the Heck Can You Freeze Anyway?' section, marked with an ice cube icon (see page 201).

Flexible-Freezing
(How to Get Your Dish Back)

While The Full Freezer Method focuses mainly on freezing individual ingredients rather than meals, you may occasionally find yourself wanting to freeze (intentional or unintentional) leftovers.

For dishes which cannot be flat-frozen or open-frozen, such as lasagne, flexible-freezing is a useful solution. This involves freezing meals in silicone bakeware, or in a serving dish lined with strong foil, so that you can remove the food from the container once it's frozen. You can then wrap it in foil and store it in a freezer bag.

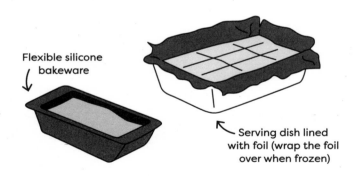

Flexible silicone bakeware

Serving dish lined with foil (wrap the foil over when frozen)

This frees up your bakeware and dishes to be used while your food is frozen, and wrapping your food without the dish means it takes up less space and is protected more effectively.

Blanching (Only Applies to Veggies)

Now, I know you're already wondering if you can skip over this bit, so I'll try to make it as painless as possible!

Basically, blanching means simply popping your veggies into boiling water for a couple of minutes and then moving them to ice-cold water to stop the veg from fully cooking. When I say ice-cold water, you don't have to use ice (I think having a lot of ice in your freezer is a waste of prime real estate) – you could just run the tap very cold or use clean ice packs to chill the water.

The time this takes varies from veggie to veggie. You'll be pleased to know that you can get away with not blanching a lot of veg, as long as you're not storing it for longer than a few months. (See the 'What the Heck Can You Freeze Anyway?' section on pages 263–6 for a summary of blanching times, and advice on which veg I strongly recommend that you *do* blanch).

Blanching is usually recommended because it helps to preserve the veg by stopping the enzymes that break down the food, so the veggies better retain their colour, flavour and texture. It's also a good safety step to ensure your veg is clean, so if you decide against blanching, make sure you give your veggies a really good wash and dry before freezing.

How to Water Blanch (aka Veggie Bath Time!)

What You'll Need:

- ☑ **Blanching basket** (optional)

- ☑ **Chopping board/sharp knife/peeler**

- ☑ **Colander**

- ☑ **Digital timer** (your phone will do!)

- ☑ **Large bowl and frozen ice packs** (or ice)

- ☑ **Lined tray** (for open-freezing)

- ☑ **Freezer bags**

- ☑ **Slotted spoon/tongs**

- ☑ **Very large saucepan** (with lid) (optional)

- ☑ **Weighing scales** (optional)

What You Need to Do . . .

Note: please read through all the steps before you start to avoid over-blanching your veggies!

1. Fill a large saucepan about two-thirds full with cold water (roughly 4.5 litres for 500 grams of veg) and set over a high heat on the hob. You want to bring the water up to a rolling boil – if you have a lid, you can put this on to help it boil faster.

2. While the water is coming to a boil, prep your veggies as you usually would (peel/trim/pod/shell/string/slice/dice). Aim for all the pieces to be roughly the same size. Place the veggies in a colander and rinse under cold running water. If you've got a large quantity, it's a good idea to weigh out 500g portions to avoid overcrowding the saucepan. You can use the same water 5–6 times to avoid having to boil fresh water each time.

3. Drop the veggies into the boiling water (or place them in a blanching basket and submerge) and bring the water back to a boil. Do not put the lid on. The water should return to a boil within a minute (use a timer to keep track). If it takes longer than a minute, take a few pieces out of the pan, then reduce the quantity when you do the next batch.

4. Once the water is boiling again, reset the timer based on the blanching times listed in the 'What the Heck Can You Freeze Anyway?' section (see pages 263–6). Meanwhile, get a bowl of ice-cold water ready (I use ice packs rather than actual ice). As soon as the timer beeps, scoop one piece of veg out and cut it in half to make sure it's piping hot throughout. If it's not, wait another 20–30 seconds and check again. Once hot, transfer your veggies using a slotted spoon or tongs straight into the ice-cold water.

5. Leave the veggies in the ice-cold water for the same amount of time as they took to blanch, then check one piece to see if it's cool throughout. If necessary, refresh the water and leave for another minute or two. Once cool, drain and dry the veggies (using kitchen paper or a clean tea towel), and open-freeze them for a few hours before bagging them up.

When it comes to using the veggies, cook them from frozen and reduce the cooking time by the number of minutes they were blanched for – just make sure they're piping hot throughout before serving.

How to Steam Blanch
(aka Veggie Spa Time!)

What You'll Need:

- ☑ Chopping board/sharp knife/peeler

- ☑ Colander

- ☑ Large bowl and frozen ice packs (or ice)

- ☑ Lined tray (for open-freezing) and freezer bags

- ☑ Steamer (or a saucepan with a tight-fitting lid and a steamer basket)

- ☑ Digital timer (your phone will do!)

- ☑ Tongs

- ☑ Weighing scales (optional)

What You Need to Do . . .

Note: please read through all the steps before you start
to avoid over-blanching your veggies!

1. Fill your steamer with water, following the
   manufacturer's instructions, and switch it on.
   Alternatively, you can add 6cm of water to a
   saucepan, along with the steaming basket, and bring
   it to a boil.

2. While the water is coming to a boil, prep your veggies
   as you usually would (peel/trim/pod/shell/string/slice/
   dice). Aim for all the pieces to be roughly the same
   size. Place the veggies in a colander and rinse under
   cold running water.

3. Once the water is boiling, place your veg in the
   compartments of the steamer in single layers and
   start the timer immediately. If you're steaming in a
   saucepan, arrange the veggies in a single layer in the
   steaming basket and put the lid on the pan. Steam
   for the amount of time advised in the 'What the Heck
   Can You Freeze Anyway?' section (see page 262).

4. Meanwhile, get a bowl of ice-cold water ready (I
   use ice packs rather than actual ice). As soon as the
   timer beeps, test one piece of veg to make sure it's

piping hot throughout. If it's not, wait another 20–30 seconds and check again. Once hot, transfer your veggies using tongs straight into the ice-cold water, being careful not to scold yourself with the steam.

5. Leave the veggies in the ice-cold water for the same amount of time as they took to blanch, then check one piece to see if it's cool throughout. If necessary, change the water and leave for another minute or two. Once cool, drain and dry the veggies (using kitchen paper or a clean tea towel), and open-freeze them for a few hours before bagging them up.

When it comes to using the veggies, cook them from frozen and reduce the cooking time by the number of minutes they were blanched for – just make sure they're piping hot throughout before serving.

Vacuum Packing

As I mentioned on pages 56–7, freezer burn happens when food becomes dehydrated. This is because the moisture is drawn out of the food and turns into ice on the food's surface and inside the freezer.

Although I'm not a fan of single-use plastics, vacuum packing is a very effective way to protect foods such as meat or fish. If your tastebuds are highly sensitive, you may want to try vacuum sealing some foods to see if it makes a difference to you. You should only ever vacuum pack foods in convenient portion sizes though, as the packs cannot be re-sealed once opened.

The most effective way to vacuum pack is with a vacuum sealer machine, which can be bought for as little as £30 online. These come with plastic pouches that you put your food in, then insert the open edge of the pouch into the machine and it sucks the air out before heat sealing the pouch closed.

If you'd like to try vacuum packing but don't want to invest in a machine, you can do this manually using a re-sealable freezer bag, a straw (I use a reusable one) and a dish of cold water. Pop your food flat inside a labelled freezer bag, place the straw inside the bag and position it along one side edge, then seal the top right up to the straw. Submerge the bag in the water, but keeping the top edge out of the water, and use the weight of water to push the air in the bag out through the straw.

Once you've removed as much air as possible, slip the straw out of the bag and seal the top. Dry off with a clean tea towel, then freeze flat so that your food takes up as little freezer space as possible.

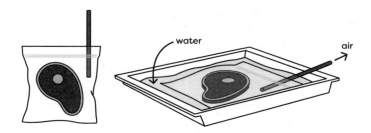

How to Make Your Freezer Space Work for You

Previously on pages 34–8, I talked about 'categorising' what foods you have in the freezer and 'containing' these so that they are grouped together with similar foods. This is a really simple and effective way to keep track of what you've got in your freezer.

I bet that the foods you already had in stock probably fell into shop-bought staples like fish fingers, chips, peas or ice cream, and maybe some home-cooked meals. There may have been a few wildcards in there too, but unless you've been following my social media for a while, it's unlikely that you had much variety in there.

Hopefully having worked through the The 5C Freezer Clear Down, you'll have already realised that you can fit far more in your freezer than you previously thought. If you haven't done this yet, flick back to page 27 and do it now.

How you want to use your freezer space going forward is completely up to you. It's likely to change over time as you test out freezing different foods to figure out what you like best and what's most useful to you. To provide a bit of inspiration, I've shared the categories that I use in my freezer on page 88 and some of the foods that fall into these categories.

The list is made up of foods that always go to waste if I don't freeze the excess and foods that I like to have in the freezer so I can throw together a quick meal. At the time of writing, I'm very lucky to have a tall integrated freezer with eight drawers, so I can designate one drawer to each category, which are clearly signposted with large vinyl labels. These labels are widely available online and can usually be customised in terms of the wording, font and

TOP TIP

If you ever need to re-label your drawers, empty the drawer out and remove it from the freezer (the food can be kept on the shelf in the freezer). Wash the drawer in warm water to get rid of any crumbs and debris. Make sure your hands are completely dry, then grab a hairdryer. Use the hot air to warm the glue on the vinyl label before peeling the label off. If there is any glue residue, use nail polish remover on a cloth to gently rub it off. Wash your drawer once more, then dry and re-label as needed!

size. Some of my freezer drawers are also carved up using simple cardboard boxes and tins, or adjustable drawer dividers. Visit www.thefullfreezer.com/freezer-tour for a video tour of my freezer.

- **Baked goods –** tortilla wraps, sliced bread, crumpets, English muffins, pancakes, homemade sandwiches, burger buns, cake, biscuits, brownies, homemade mini quiche

- **Cooked meats & leftovers –** cooked chicken, cooked gammon, cooked sausages, chorizo, pepperoni, ham, Bolognese, lasagne, risotto, tomato soup, cooked pasta, cooked rice, Spanish omelette, hummus, guacamole, cooked burgers, red wine, white wine

- **Fruit –** raspberries, strawberries, blueberries, mango, grapes, banana, pineapple, cherries, orange slices, lemon slices and wedges, lime slices and wedges, stewed rhubarb

- **Dairy –** milk, single cream, double cream, homemade flavoured butters, Parmesan, homemade white sauce, ice cream, torn mozzarella, grated cheddar

- **Veggies –** white onion, red onion, peppers, sweetcorn, sweet potato wedges and chips, mashed potato, roast potatoes, jacket potatoes, spring onions, cherry tomatoes, courgettes, chestnut mushrooms, fennel, butternut squash, rosemary, basil, thyme, ginger, garlic, chillies, corn on the cob, mangetout, parsley, leeks, grated carrots, diced carrots, carrot batons, chives, lemongrass purée, celery, broccoli, cauliflower

- **Pantry items –** pesto, tomato purée, coconut milk, tinned tomatoes, kidney beans, black beans, olives, cashew nuts, pine nuts, white wine vinegar, mustard, teriyaki sauce, salsa, chickpeas, hoisin sauce, satay sauce, sesame seeds, walnuts, pumpkin seeds, chia seeds, ground almonds, pineapple juice, passata, sultanas, mango chutney

- **Fish & seafood –** white fish fillets, salmon fillets, seabass, fish fingers, breaded fish, tuna steaks, prawns

- **Raw meat –** chicken thighs, chicken breasts (butterflied), chicken nuggets, beef mince, pork mince, lamb mince, sausages, burgers

Hopefully my list of categories has got you thinking about just how much you could have stocked in your freezer. However, you might be starting to wonder if you can freeze some foods that *aren't* on this list . . .

The truth is, almost everything can be frozen, you just need to know the best way to do it, whether that's open-freezing, flat-freezing or cube-freezing.

To demonstrate just how much you can freeze, I've included a section at the end of this book called 'What the Heck Can You Freeze Anyway?' (see pages 197–300). This takes you through how to freeze a raft of different foods. If a food isn't in there, it doesn't mean that it can't be frozen – have a look to see if there's something similar listed and try it out!

And if you're really not sure about whether a particular food can be frozen, give me a shout @TheFullFreezer on Instagram or Facebook, I'm always happy to experiment with freezing more foods!

TOP TIP

Often shops label foods as 'not suitable for home freezing'. Rather than it being a safety risk, this is usually because it impacts the quality of the food, so it may need to be used in a different way to normal.

It's always worth dropping the manufacturer a line (via email, phone or social media) to ask if the food shouldn't be frozen because of safety or quality reasons. Sometimes it might be because the food contains ingredients that have previously been frozen and defrosted (such as pizza toppings), in which case you shouldn't freeze them; but in a lot of cases, it'll be safe to freeze your food for another day.

A Simple Way to Get Started

The simplest way to start building your Freezer Stash is to freeze anything that previously would have ended up in the bin, as long as you know it's something that you'll actually use (remember The Five Golden Rules on pages 54–8).

Every time something is at risk of going to waste, prep it using the guidance in this book and stash it in the freezer instead. The beauty of this approach is that there's no need for lengthy prep sessions in the kitchen. You can chop up those spare peppers in the pack while you cook tonight's dinner, or give that bag of carrots to your significant other to chop in front of the TV. If you've got kids, you could even get them to help with prepping and organising the food for the freezer.

If you do find yourself with quite a lot of fresh stuff all going out of date at once, it's best to freeze a few things at a time (each item should only take a few hours) rather than everything at once. Putting lots of fresh food in the freezer at once will raise the temperature and things won't freeze as quickly.

As you start to build up this Freezer Stash of rescued fresh foods, you'll most likely need to revisit how you are categorising the food in your freezer; this is all part of the process of building a Freezer Stash that truly works for you.

This approach to building your Freezer Stash can be super satisfying financially too, particularly once you start to build up enough ingredients to be able to cook full meals. There's nothing I love more than feeling like I've made a meal essentially for free!

Buying Reduced and in Bulk

If you're keen to build up your Freezer Stash fairly quickly, you could buy ingredients that you use a lot of to purposefully stock your freezer. Do remember that it's best not to freeze too much all at once though.

Ingredients that I always have in stock include sliced onions, peppers, ginger, garlic, and a selection of meats; these are flat-frozen or open-frozen in small pieces so they can be defrosted quickly.

If you're looking to make savings on your food bill, you could take advantage of supermarket special offers on meat, fish and veggies – look out for any 'yellow-sticker' reductions. Just try not to get carried away!

It's worth finding out at your local shop where they stock their reduced foods and what time of day they start to make reductions. Armed with this information, you can take advantage of all sorts of savings; pop your spoils straight into the freezer (after portioning them up or open-freezing them, of course).

TOP TIP

Although it's best to freeze food while it's as fresh as possible, you can freeze it right up until the use-by date. Even if a product says 'freeze on the day of purchase', as long as you've stored it correctly and it's not showing any signs of spoilage, food can still be frozen up until the use-by date. Be sure to cook it promptly once defrosted though, and if possible, cook it from frozen.

By shopping reduced-sticker foods, not only can you save yourself some cash, but you'll also be doing something great for the planet by ensuring these foods don't end up in landfill, along with their packaging. It's also well worth checking out apps to bag yourself some freebies or bargains (Olio and Too Good to Go are great for this), just be wary of 'magic bags' filled with foods that can't be frozen. If possible, query whether the food inside has been cooked fresh, or reheated, and whether it's previously been frozen.

Quick Fixes

For those who want to use their freezer more effectively but are time-poor, I really encourage you to sweep through your local supermarket freezer aisle (or have a gander online). Yes, The Full Freezer Method is all about freezing fresh foods, but it doesn't mean you can't go for convenience and buy pre-prepped frozen produce too!

If you haven't had a look recently, you'll be amazed by the range of products available these days. The freezer section isn't all about processed foods, in fact, because freezing is a natural preservative, you can get stacks of ready-to-cook ingredients that don't have anything added to them. There are all sorts of fruits, veggies, herbs, meat and fish available these days, many of which can be cooked straight from frozen.

My two complaints about pre-frozen foods are the quantities that they come in and the way they're sometimes prepared before freezing. For example, frozen spinach is a bargain, but I find the cubes are bulky and the size of the pack is larger than necessary. Pre-chopped frozen peppers tend to frustrate me too, as they're cut small and disappear to nothing when cooked – not an issue if you're cooking soup, but not great for a stir fry.

It's worth bearing in mind that frozen prepped veggies aren't always cheaper than buying fresh and prepping your own. But, if you usually buy ready-prepped fresh produce and end up wasting some, then frozen ready-prepped might be a more cost-effective option for you.

IMPORTANT: CHECK THE PACKAGING

If you buy frozen foods, always check the packaging to see if it needs cooking before eating. For example, products such as sweetcorn or spinach may need cooking to make them safe, so you can't just defrost them and add them to your salad or smoothie.

When it comes to buying frozen prepped food, the key is to simply give things a go. Ditch the pre-conceived ideas you most likely have about frozen foods and experiment with them.

You'll gradually get a sense of what works well for you, and what you would prefer to prep and freeze yourself. And if you buy a product and decide you're not keen, remember to pass it on or use it up as quickly as possible so it doesn't end up living in your freezer for ages (soup is always a good option!). Be sure to check out the cooking tips in the next section of this book to get the most from your ingredients.

How Long Can I Freeze For?

I have lost count of the number of times I've been asked how long foods can be frozen. It's a sensible question, after all, many of us have grown up in an era of use-by and best before dates and are nervous about consuming anything beyond the labelled date.

You should, of course, follow the guidance on the food packaging (see pages 193–4 for more on the difference between best before and use-by dates). When it comes to freezing, technically your food could last indefinitely as long as:

- **it was properly cared for before freezing**

- **it was kept consistently cold enough during freezing**

- **it is safely defrosted and cooked**

This is because harmful bacteria cannot multiply at very low temperatures.

The longer a food is frozen, however, the more the quality will degrade, and if it has not been sufficiently protected from the cold, freezer burn may damage the quality so much that you won't be so keen on eating it.

Generally speaking, if the food appears to be okay and you've followed the safety guidelines (we cover these shortly, on page 101), then it'll most likely be absolutely fine to eat.

On the flip side, if something you've frozen smells or tastes funny, it's best not to risk it, even if you're confident that you've followed all the rules. A good rule of thumb is to use most foods within 3–6 months, or within 1 month if it's something small or delicate that's likely to become freezer burned easily, such as thinly sliced cooked meats. Rather than immediately throwing foods away after this time, use your senses and your judgement to determine whether it's safe to eat older foods.

If you've previously been guilty of stowing foods away in your freezer for way too long, I hope your newfound love of freezing is going to help you keep on top of your Freezer Stash and start seeing your freezer as a pause button for food rather than long-term storage!

TAKE ACTION

Right. Let's set some more intentions before we move on to the cooking. Use the space below to jot down how you're going to begin building your Freezer Stash. Could you even go and freeze something from the fridge, right now, to get you started? See the 'What the Heck Can You Freeze Anyway?' section (page 197) to find out how!

....

....

....

....

....

....

PHASE 4:
Using Your Freezer Stash

Huzzah! You've done it . . . your freezer is organised *and* you've started to build your Freezer Stash. It might just be small at the moment, but that's okay. The important thing is that you've taken the first steps. If you haven't started yet, what are you playing at?! Take a look in your fridge and see if there's anything you could save from the bin today.

If you've started to build up your Freezer Stash, then you're ready for the next step as there's no point in storing all this food if you're not going to use it!

In this phase, I'm going to talk you through cooking tricks and techniques to make the most of your frozen food, the food safety rules you need to follow and some of the scenarios in which your freezer can become your very best friend. Let's do this!

Three Commandments to Keep You Safe

Before we get stuck into the cooking methods, there are a few food safety rules you need to know. Please don't skip over this section (unless you're already food safety trained), because understanding these key points will keep you and your family safe. This advice will also give you the confidence to know what food is okay to eat and what should go in the bin (because reducing food waste should never put anyone's health at risk!).

1. **Cool Quickly** This relates to any leftovers from cooked meals that are heading into the fridge or freezer (regardless of whether the ingredients have or haven't been previously frozen).

I'll be honest with you, I unknowingly used to break this rule *so often* when I used to batch cook. I loved lining up all of the meals that I'd prepared before transferring them to the freezer at once (which I also shouldn't have done!). When I was batch cooking, food could sit out on the kitchen counter for up to 12 hours.

This might explain why I had all sorts of gastric distress back in the day. I spent months going through an elimination diet in my twenties to identify what was causing my tummy troubles; it turns out I might have just been giving myself food poisoning!

So, why is it important that we cool our food down quickly? Well, when food is warm (between 8°C and 63°C – i.e. warmer than your fridge and cooler than your oven) it's the perfect breeding ground for harmful bacteria.

By cooling food down within two hours (or one hour for high-risk food such as rice), you reduce the risk of that bacteria multiplying and the food making you sick.

This DOES NOT mean putting hot or warm food straight into the fridge or freezer.

If warm food is put in the fridge or freezer, the internal temperature of the appliance is raised, which puts other food at risk.

Also, although doing this may cool down the outside of the food faster, the food in the middle of the dish is likely to sit at an unsafe temperature, encouraging harmful bacteria to multiply.

What's the best way to cool your food down quickly?

- Stir regularly or spread out in a large dish so that the heat can escape

- Split into small portions

- If plain (such as rice or pasta), place in a sieve and rinse under cold running water

- Place the food in a dish, in an ice bath (particularly useful for dishes such as lasagne that can't be stirred!)

When you're cooling your food at room temperature, it's also a good idea to keep it under a mesh food tent to protect it from any bugs or other nasties.

2. **Don't Defrost at Room Temperature** I know, I know. You might well have been doing this for the last 20 or 30 years (or longer!), and you may be thinking 'well, it's never made me sick!' If you've *ever* had an unexplained fever, diarrhoea, nausea, stomach cramps or even just felt tired or unwell, these

symptoms could be down to something you've eaten. Also, contrary to popular belief, food poisoning doesn't always mean projectile vomiting, and it doesn't always happen immediately; symptoms can occur days, weeks and even months later.

IMPORTANT: CHILLED FOOD

It's important to keep the temperature in mind when serving 'chilled' foods too. How long they are safe for out of the fridge will depend on the food and how warm the environment is. The best option is to keep these foods out of direct sunlight and return them to the fridge as soon as you're able. It's important to remember that foods should only be left out of the fridge like this once, and if they're left out for more than four hours they should be thrown away. This is different to the two-hour rule for hot foods (see page 102) as it takes longer for cold food to warm up to an unsafe temperature (8 - 63°C).

Certain people are more vulnerable to contracting food poisoning; so, although *you* might not get sick, young children, elderly people, pregnant women and those with a compromised immune system are far more likely to suffer these symptoms, or worse. Check out page 109 for how to defrost your food safely.

So, why shouldn't you defrost at room temperature? Well, the science supporting this is exactly the same as for rule one (see page 102). If food is left to sit at room temperature (or rather, between 8°C and 63°C – referred to by food safety experts as 'The Danger Zone'), harmful bacteria will start to multiply. And if you're leaving frozen food out to defrost, the chances are that you'll be leaving it out at that temperature for quite a while, giving that bacteria ample opportunity to grow.

Of course, it depends on what the food is. For example, foods usually kept at room temperature, such as bread, will be fine (more about defrosting these later on page 223), but any foods that are usually chilled need to be kept cool while they defrost.

Won't cooking kill the bacteria anyway? Although cooking frozen food until it's piping hot throughout is a great precaution when it comes to ensuring your food is safe (this is the third food safety commandment), unfortunately it isn't a silver bullet. If you've allowed harmful bacteria to develop, cooking should kill them off, *but* the dying bacteria can release spores which contain poisonous toxins that may make you really sick. Cooking will not destroy these toxins, and there are cases where these have caused serious illness and even death.

3. **Cook Until Piping Hot** Have you guessed what I'm going to say here? Yep, this is all to do with that pesky food safety 'Danger Zone' (see page 102) again! If you just warm up frozen food, instead of getting it piping hot throughout, you're literally creating the perfect environment for harmful bacteria to develop. Because freezing doesn't kill bacteria, you need to heat food all the way up to a safe temperature for a sufficient amount of time (see the table below for the UK Food Standards Agency's recommended time/ temperature combinations).

SAFE FOOD TEMPERATURE VS TIME

TEMPERATURE	TIME
60°C	45 minutes
65°C	10 minutes
70°C	2 minutes
75°C	30 seconds
80°C	6 seconds

Remember, this is particularly important if you're heating through food for anyone vulnerable – young children, elderly people, pregnant women and those with compromised immune systems.

To give you the absolute confidence that you've heated your food thoroughly enough, I really recommend investing in a food probe thermometer (see pages 60–1). To use these correctly, you need to insert the probe into the thickest part of your food, or

TOP TIP

The best way to keep your family's food free of harmful bacteria is to always follow the instructions on the packaging, including not eating foods after the use-by date (see pages 193–4 for more about use-by vs best before dates). If you know you're not going to eat something before the use-by date, make sure you store it correctly and freeze it before or on the use-by date.

the largest piece. Remember, if the food is not up to a safe temperature, you'll need to clean and disinfect the probe before testing your food again. This can be done using hot water and soap (only clean the probe, not the whole thermometer), and then submerge the probe in boiling water for one minute.

So, how can you safely defrost your food (and ensure it's defrosted in time for dinner)? First of all, I want to remind you that not all foods actually need defrosting before cooking or reheating (see pages 57–8), particularly if you follow The Full Freezer Method of freezing. This advice only really applies to frozen meat (although I do also share how you can safely cook meat from frozen on pages 122–3) or if you want to defrost a large cooked meal to speed up the reheating process and ensure it reheats evenly.

Three Safe Ways to Defrost

1. In The Fridge

This is by far the safest option as it will ensure the food stays as cold as possible, it is however also the slowest.

You should always defrost on the bottom shelf of the fridge, in a container to avoid any drips or spillages from the defrosting food (see pages 34–6 for advice on how to safely stock your fridge).

The general rule regarding the time it takes to defrost in the fridge is 10 – 12 hours per kilogram of meat.

Once this food is defrosted, it should be cooked as soon as possible, and always within 24 hours.

2. In Cold Water

You will be amazed how much faster food defrosts when it is submerged in cold water! It can reduce days to hours, and hours to minutes.

If necessary, you can use a cup or bowl to weigh the food down. The difference between this and defrosting in the fridge is that you cannot just leave your food overnight.

If submerged in a dish of cold water you'll need to refresh the water every 30 minutes, or you may prefer to leave the dish in the sink with the tap running ever so slightly so that the water is constantly being refreshed.

3. Microwave

The most important thing when defrosting food in the microwave is that you cook it immediately without allowing it to cool (and it absolutely should NOT be returned to the fridge after microwaving).

This is because when you microwave it you start to increase the temperature, putting your food into the 'Danger Zone' (8 – 60°C). The only reason that this is okay, is because the microwave defrosts so quickly that there isn't time for bad bacteria to multiply.

As long as you continue to raise the temperature of the food and get it cooked quickly your food will be safe to eat.

*'But hang on a minute, Kate . . . Didn't you
say I could ditch defrosting?'*

Well, yes, I did (see pages 57–8). *However*, in some
circumstances, defrosting is necessary. For example, it's
always preferable to defrost meat (unless it's 'cook from
frozen'), especially large joints, so that you can cook the
meat to a safe temperature without overcooking it. Also,
if you're planning to slow cook, it's vital that you defrost
all of your ingredients first (unless it's something small like
peas that are thrown in towards the end of the cooking
time). More on this later (see page 120). Just to be clear
(because I hear this one a lot), it's not okay to defrost
food by submerging it in hot water! Remember, we need
to keep our food cold to avoid those harmful bacteria
developing.

Why the 'sniff test' isn't always enough

It drives me mad when I hear people talking about giving
their food a quick 'sniff' to check if it's okay. Don't get me
wrong, this is fine if it's a best before-date food, such as
fruit or veg (see page 193), but it's rare that anyone would
sniff these to check their quality as you can usually tell
simply by looking at them.

The reality is that most people sniff food when it's

meat or something else with a use-by date. The problem with this is that there are two types of bacteria, and the one that makes foods dangerous can't be seen or smelt. Understanding the difference between these two types of bacteria was a real 'penny-drop' moment for me, so I hope it'll be the same for you.

1. **Pathogenic Bacteria** This is basically the 'bad' bacteria that I've previously referred to. Most likely you've already heard of E-Coli O157, Salmonella and Listeria. These are all types of bacteria that can make us sick, but they're not the same as the bacteria that make our food rot. This means that it's possible for some foods to look, smell and even taste okay even though it contains unsafe levels of pathogenic bacteria.

2. **Spoilage Bacteria** This is what makes our food rot or smell. Although the thought of eating food that's starting to rot might turn your stomach, these bacteria are far less likely to make you poorly than their pathogenic (silent-but-deadly) counterparts!

IMPORTANT: DON'T RISK IT

We can be carriers and spreaders of different bacteria ourselves, so you should never freeze foods or drinks that have been partially consumed. For example, you could freeze leftover coffee from a cafetière, but you shouldn't freeze leftover coffee from a mug that has been drunk from. If there's any risk that our bacteria has contaminated the leftover food, it's better to bin it.

Becoming a Freezer Stash Master

The most important thing to understand when it comes to cooking using frozen ingredients is that often you'll not be able to use them in the same way that you would if they weren't frozen.

For example, you can't freeze a salad and then defrost it to eat as a salad, but you could freeze the individual parts of a salad and then use the tomatoes in a Bolognese or pasta sauce, add the lettuce to smoothies or soups or cook the peppers in stir fries or curries.

Likewise, if you freeze banana slices, you won't want to defrost them and eat them like a fresh banana because they'll turn into a disgusting grey mush. You can, however, eat them frozen (dip them in dark chocolate for a surprisingly delicious and healthy choc ice) or whizz them into a soft scoop ice cream.

One of the questions I'm asked most often is whether it's 'safe' to freeze specific foods. What you need to know is that it's not dangerous to freeze food (you must look after it correctly before and after freezing though). All that freezing does is turn any water in the food into ice and lowers the internal temperature so that any bacteria in the food cannot multiply (it doesn't kill it though, which is why we need to be careful when defrosting).

As the water in the food turns into ice, it expands, which means the cell walls in the food can become broken. This is why so many foods turn to mush when you defrost them after freezing. When you freeze food quickly, smaller ice crystals form and less damage is done to the cell walls, better helping to preserve the quality of your food. This is one of the reasons why I love open-freezing, as those small pieces of food freeze so much faster than a massive clump!

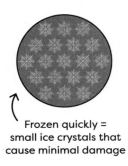

**Frozen quickly =
small ice crystals that
cause minimal damage**

**Frozen slowly=
big ice crystals that
damage cell walls**

Some foods contain only a little water, so they can be
defrosted and used as if fresh (for example bread), but
most will need to be cooked in some way or consumed
straight from frozen.

I explain this in more depth in relation to specific
foods in the 'What the Heck Can You Freeze Anyway?'
section on page 197, but I've also provided some tips
on the following pages, sharing ways to cook using your
Freezer Stash to get the best possible results.

Remember, if you're not sure if a food can be
defrosted and then treated as if fresh, there's nothing
stopping you from defrosting one piece (assuming that
it was open-frozen), to see how it behaves. As long as
you defrost safely, that's all that really matters – how
acceptable the texture and taste are after freezing really
comes down to personal preference.

The Key to Freezer Stash Cooking

As I said earlier, there's no point in freezing food if you're never going to eat it. By ensuring that ingredients are prepped and frozen with their end use in mind (see page 53), Freezer Stash cooking is incredibly convenient, with some foods cooking even faster from frozen than they do from fresh. Cooking with frozen ingredients is a little bit different to cooking with fresh, however, so it's important to understand how to use your Freezer Stash once it's frozen.

So, what do you need to know about cooking using your Freezer Stash?

These are the five things that you need to keep in mind:

1. Most foods can be cooked or reheated straight from frozen (see page 57)

2. You may need to start cooking frozen foods on a high heat to evaporate off excess moisture

3. Some frozen foods may cook faster than you expect

4. Frozen ingredients must not be left sat at room temperature

5. The food must be piping hot throughout before serving (see page 106)

As long as you take care of your food properly before you freeze it, and you make sure anything cooked is heated to a safe temperature (see page 106), there's no reason that you can't experiment with your Freezer Stash cooking.

Remember Golden Rule 3: Tweak and Try Again; if you cook a frozen food using a particular method and find you're not keen on it, consider whether you could try a different approach. For example, I'm not a big fan of frozen carrot slices that have been boiled (I don't love fresh ones either!), but I could eat frozen carrot batons that have been roasted all day long!

Now, if you're wondering, can I cook up a Freezer Stash meal using any cooking method, the answer is *almost* (see the Slow Cooking section on pages 120-1).

Generally speaking, heat is applied to the food pretty quickly during cooking so it goes from being frozen to cooked in relatively little time. This is great because it means that any harmful bacteria that has been lying dormant in the food doesn't have the opportunity to multiply to a dangerous level.

To give you more confidence around using your Freezer Stash with your preferred cooking method, I've shared some tips below. And remember, it's perfectly okay to mix fresh and frozen ingredients, so you can dip into your Stash for just a few ingredients, or you could whip up a whole meal – the choice is yours!

Cooking on the hob/stove

This is one of my favourite ways to cook using my Freezer Stash. It's so easy to throw in a handful of this and that to whip up dinner in a flash.

If you're frying vegetables, you'll need to evaporate off the excess moisture quite quickly before turning the heat down. To do this, get your pan and oil nice and hot, then add your frozen ingredients. I always fry sliced onions and any 'dense' ingredients such as carrots first, then add lighter ingredients such as mushrooms or peppers.

You will most likely notice a plume of steam as the excess moisture evaporates. You'll need to keep stirring your food to help this steam escape. Once your food no longer appears to be frozen, and all the excess moisture has evaporated, you can turn the heat down and continue to cook as normal.

If you skip this initial step, your veggies will likely end up stewing in the water they've released and lose all their bite.

When boiling or steaming, reduce the cooking time by the amount of time the veg was blanched for before freezing, otherwise you may overcook it (see page 80).

If you're using frozen 'wet' ingredients such as coconut milk or tinned tomatoes, these can be added to your dish straight from the freezer, but you may need to pop a lid onto the pan for a bit to help them defrost and reheat faster. If you're concerned about your dish overcooking, you might want to defrost these 'wet' ingredients overnight in the fridge or in a dish of cold water before adding them. You could also defrost them in the microwave if you're using them immediately.

Remember that you need to ensure everything is piping hot throughout before serving, so consider investing in a food probe thermometer (see pages 60–1) to make sure everything is up to a safe temperature before dishing up!

Cooking in the oven

Lots of frozen foods cook beautifully in the oven. It's possible to cook an entire roast dinner straight from frozen (and yes, that goes for Christmas dinner too!)

As with hob cooking, you may find some foods release excess water – for example, when you roast frozen tomatoes. This isn't a problem if you're making something like a soup or a casserole, but if it's a traybake, you're best to use fresh ingredients. If you don't have fresh, you can use frozen, but I recommend roasting them on a separate tray from your other veggies initially. This will stop your other ingredients from becoming wet, and allow you to drain off the excess liquid before adding the tomatoes to your main dish.

The key to making sure your oven-roasted vegetables reheat evenly is to spread them out on a baking tray so that they're not touching each other. Before roasting, toss the veggies in a little oil and season them with salt and pepper or coat them in spices such as paprika or a Cajun blend (you can make your own or buy these ready-made), which is a great way to enhance their flavour. If you're cooking foods such as potato wedges, putting the skin-side face down on the tray will help each piece to crisp up better than if laid on their side.

Always preheat the oven, so the excess moisture in your food can be quickly evaporated off. However, you do not need to cook on a higher heat in the oven just because your ingredients are frozen – as a general rule, they should not take much longer to cook. The exception to this is if you are cooking or reheating a dish you have prepared and frozen, such as lasagne or cottage pie. In this case, you need to add at least 50 per cent longer to the cooking time and ensure the food is piping hot throughout (I recommend using a food probe thermometer – see pages 60–1). It's also super important that you make sure the dish or container used is safe to go straight from the freezer to the oven too, as it may otherwise shatter!

As I mentioned on page 110, it's a good idea to defrost meat before cooking so you can make sure it cooks evenly throughout. However, I do want to flag up that many supermarkets now sell 'cook from frozen' meats. These have been appropriately tested to ensure they can be cooked safely in a domestic oven straight from frozen – they're brilliant if you find you're always on the back foot with defrosting meat!

Cooking in a slow cooker

This is a *very* important topic for us to touch on because you should <u>never</u> put frozen foods in a slow cooker (no, not even veggies).

This is because slow cookers work at a low temperature, and do not bring food up to a safe temperature (above The Danger Zone – see page 105) fast enough. The only exception to this is if you're adding something very small or fine (e.g. frozen peas or spinach) towards the end of the cooking time when the dish is already piping hot.

This doesn't mean that you can't slow cook at all though. You simply need to defrost your ingredients first in the fridge or fry them up in a pan before adding them to your slow cooker.

My preference is always for the latter, as it allows you to evaporate off any excess water and many slow cookers now come with a hob-safe insert, meaning you don't even need to do any extra washing up! Remember that you don't need to fully cook the ingredients before they go into the slow cooker, you just need them to be thawed. Just be sure to preheat your slow cooker so the food's temperature continues to rise.

If you do choose to defrost your ingredients before slow cooking (an approach favoured by those who like making 'dump bags' – see page 131 for more about these), you might need to remove the lid for the last 30–60 minutes of cooking to allow the excess liquid to evaporate or add a thickening agent such as cornflour.

Cooking in a pressure cooker

The pressure cooker isn't a particularly common piece of kit here in the UK, but it's the perfect match for frozen foods and so I *had* to include a section on pressure cooking. Although you can get traditional pressure cookers for use on the hob, nowadays there are far more sophisticated appliances on the market, called multi-cookers.

It can take a little bit of work to get to grips with a multi-cooker, but once you get comfortable using one, they're a game changer. I learnt to use mine with the help of Jenny Tschiesche @lunchboxdoctor and can very much recommend her books and social media to get you started!

What I love about these is that they usually have a sauté function, so you can brown meat and fry veggies before pressure cooking. If necessary, you can then use the same function to evaporate off any excess liquid at the end of the cooking process. Many multi-cookers even include an air-frying function now, so you can pressure cook your dish and then crisp it up all in the same pot.

What's even more genius is that you can safely cook meat and fish straight from frozen in a multi-cooker. And I'm not just talking about little pieces – you can cook a whole frozen joint of meat! As long as it will fit in the pot, you can cook it in the multi-cooker. Simply pour about 200ml water or stock into the base of the pot, rest the meat above it on a trivet and cook for 16 ½ minutes per 500g, then allow the pot to release pressure naturally. I've managed to cook a 750g turkey crown straight from frozen in less than an hour, so I know it works!

The reason why this is possible in a pressure cooker is because the food cooks through so quickly under such high pressure that there's no time for harmful bacteria to develop. And because the food is being cooked using pressurised steam, it won't end up burnt on the outside and raw in the middle (although it is possible to overcook it, if you're not careful).

Just be sure to check all cooked meat with a food probe thermometer before serving (see pages 60–1). If you find the meat in the pressure cooker is not quite cooked through, you can always pop it back on for a few more minutes.

If you'd like a quick reference cheat sheet for cooking lots of different foods in a pressure cooker, both fresh and frozen, there is a magnetic one listed in my Amazon shop (www.amazon.co.uk/shop/thefullfreezer).

Cooking in an air fryer

If you don't already own an air fryer, all you really need to know is that essentially they're just a really powerful mini oven. They're far more efficient than a conventional oven though, so they're great for your electricity bills and for hungry tummies that need feeding as soon as possible.

Much the same as with an oven, you can absolutely cook from frozen in an air fryer – the rules to follow are quite similar. Always preheat your air fryer before cooking frozen foods and make sure that items are spread out in a single layer so the air can circulate around each piece of food. An air fryer rack with two or three shelves is a useful investment as it means you can cook your food in layers all at the same time see my Amazon shop (www.amazon.co.uk/shop/thefullfreezer).

The main difference between air fryers and conventional ovens is that the heat in an air fryer is far more intense than an oven, so you don't need to cook at as high temperature or for as long.

The recommended conversion rule (thanks again to Jenny Tschiesche @lunchboxdoctor) that you should follow is either:

- **Use the recommended conventional oven temperature (not the fan oven temperature), but reduce the cooking time by half**

- **Or if the recommended conventional oven temperature is too high for your air fryer's range,**

cook at 20°C less (usually the same as the recommended fan oven temperature) and reduce the cooking time by 25 per cent.

When cooking in an air fryer, Jenny also recommends adding some moisture to any non-breaded frozen foods, which could be a little oil, butter or slices of fresh citrus. Wrapping foods like frozen fish in foil helps to keep them lovely and moist, whilst ensuring they cook through thoroughly. Avoid using any low-calorie spray oils in your air fryer as they can damage the non-stick surfaces. Olive oil, coconut oil or avocado oil stored in a spray bottle is a much better option.

The real joy of the air fryer is that it's so easy to check your food while it's cooking and to adjust the time and temperature as necessary. Use a food probe thermometer and once it's up to a safe temperature (see page 106), you're good to go!

Cooking in a microwave

I'll be honest with you, when it comes to cooking from scratch, the microwave isn't my first choice, *but* I do use it regularly for defrosting and reheating foods.

Your microwave should have a defrost setting (usually around 20–30 per cent power). If it doesn't, I strongly recommend digging out the manual (they're usually available online if you can't find the original).

Knowing how to defrost food safely using your specific model of microwave is a *really* handy skill to have – it's well worth the three minutes it takes to check. Your instruction manual may also give advice on the recommended timings for defrosting or cooking/ reheating specific foods, and some have preprogrammed functions to take all of the guesswork out of it!

Remember it's important what containers you use in the microwave – please, please, please do not put freezer bags in there unless they specifically say they're suitable for microwaving. The best option is a microwave-safe round dish with straight sides as this helps the food to defrost and reheat more evenly.

When it comes to reheating or cooking in a microwave, the most important thing is to ensure that your food reaches a safe temperature (see page 106) and that there aren't any cold spots.

The best way to do this (if possible) is to stir it halfway through cooking, then allow your food to rest for a few minutes before serving. This allows the heat to dissipate and warm the food more evenly. Of course, your food probe thermometer (see pages 60–1) is your best friend in this situation!

Freezer Stash to The Rescue

When you're first getting started with your Freezer Stash, you might find it easiest to stick to recipes you're familiar with and just switch out a handful of ingredients from fresh to frozen. For example, using frozen garlic, frozen herbs or frozen leftover passata.

I absolutely love it when I go to cook a meal using fresh ingredients, realise I don't have everything I need but then remember the missing ingredients are in the freezer. It's a satisfying feeling once you know you've got that ingredient you need right there, ready to use straight from frozen.

Think about the recipes that you cook regularly (or are most familiar with) to identify whether there are usually any leftover ingredients. If you did the exercise on page 26, you might already have a pretty good idea of what those ingredients are.

Use the space on page 128 to jot these down, and then have a nosy at 'What the Heck Can You Freeze Anyway?' (see page 197) to see if you can start freezing these foods for another day.

LEFTOVER INGREDIENTS I ALWAYS END UP CHUCKING AWAY

....

....

....

....

Full Freezer Stash Meals

When you're building your Freezer Stash, there comes a point when you have enough ingredients to cook a whole meal. I'm not talking about fish fingers and chips, I'm talking about curries, stir-fries, roasts and much more.

Whenever I chat with people about freezer food, it's understandable that their minds go straight to those typical freezer products, but there's *so* much more that can be cooked from frozen if you have a variety of ingredients to hand.

What I want you to know is that you could pick up almost any recipe book off your shelf at home and use frozen ingredients in the place of fresh.

Of course, if the recipe is for a salad, frozen ingredients won't fix your dinnertime hankering (unless you want to roast them and serve them with fresh salad leaves), but when it comes to cooked dishes, your Freezer Stash should be able to help you out.

If you haven't already read the cooking tips in 'The Key to Freezer Stash Cooking' (see page 115), it's worth checking those out before you dive in. You really can give anything a go though – cooking is all about experimentation, so don't be afraid to find out what works for you!

The Full Freezer Loves . . .

In case you haven't already realised, the real joy of The Full Freezer Method is its flexibility. Although there are specific tricks and techniques that will help you make the most of your space, and make freezing more convenient, the circumstances that you use them under can vary massively from home to home.

I love it when I'm chatting to someone who thinks The Full Freezer Method 'isn't for them', only to come up with the perfect way for it to make their life easier and less wasteful. To help you identify how the process can best work for you, I've summarised some typical scenarios below. I hope these will inspire you to put what you've learnt into practice as soon as possible!

Skip to the bits that you feel are most relevant to you, but do give the rest a quick look too in case there are any tips you could share with friends or family. And remember, how you use your freezer is likely to change over time, so while one approach may not work for you right now, it might be useful knowledge for the future.

. . . Batch Cooking

Seeing as this used to be completely my bag, it feels like a good place to start! If you love batch cooking, I totally get it. It worked well for me for over a decade. Without a doubt, it's a total lifesaver on those nights when cooking from scratch just isn't an option.

There are a few ways in which The Full Freezer Method can support your batch cooking:

- **Freezing leftover ingredients (such as garlic, chilli and ginger) so they can be used for future batching sessions or general cooking.** These are so handy to have in stock – you can buy them ready-prepped from the supermarket freezer aisle, if you prefer.

- **Freeze other surplus ingredients that you usually just throw into your dish, even though it's more than you need (such as mushrooms, carrots or leeks).** Although adding them to your cooking is a great way to avoid any waste, it does mean you may end up with excessive amounts of one dish, which can get pretty boring. If you freeze those four mushrooms, three carrots or that single leek instead, they can be used in other dishes (for example, on pizzas, in pasta dishes and in stir-fries).

- **If you have limited time available to batch cook, you could separate the preparation from the cooking (or even use some ready-prepped shop-bought frozen ingredients).** It's perfectly fine to use frozen ingredients to cook with and then freeze the cooked dish (see 'The Full Freezer Loop' on page 17) as long as the frozen ingredients haven't previously been cooked (such as frozen cooked chicken). Some people like to freeze the ingredients for a single meal all together in one freezer bag (referred to as a 'dump bag'). These don't work for me right now as I would rather not be tied to having specific meals in the freezer, but if you want to be confident you've got everything you need in one bag, this can be a really useful approach. They usually need to be defrosted in the fridge in advance though. If this sounds good to you, check out @TheBatchLady for stacks of grab-and-go inspiration.

- **If you're adding a new meal to your batch cooking rotation, you can cook a small quantity and test**

out freezing it. Any surplus ingredients can then be frozen either to make the same meal (if you like it) or something different. Why bother doing this? Well, as I flagged up on page 54, you should avoid ever freezing something that you don't actually like. I've made the mistake in the past of introducing new recipes without doing a test run, then if they turned out to be a disappointment, they ended up buried at the back of the freezer. A waste of food, as well as a waste of freezer space.

- **Consider flat-freezing your batch-cooked meals, just as you do for ingredients like tinned tomatoes and coconut milk.** This will take up much less freezer space and also means that you don't need to take them out in advance to defrost. A quick run under the cold tap makes it easy to remove the food from the bag and then reheat straight from frozen.

For me, this has eliminated those 'well-intentioned' situations when I remove something from the freezer to defrost and then plans change. If this ever happens to you, you have 24 hours to eat the food, from the point that the food is defrosted. If your food hasn't fully thawed and still has plenty of ice crystals then you're fine to pop it back in the freezer.

One thing I must point out in relation to batch cooking (or 'dump bag' prep) is that you need to be careful about how much fresh food you're freezing in one go. When I used to batch cook, I would load all of my freshly cooked meals into the freezer all at once. What I didn't realise was that my freezer had to work a lot harder to maintain the cold temperature and my food would have frozen very slowly – allowing harmful bacteria the chance to develop and impacting the quality.

Ideally, you shouldn't be loading your freezer with more than 10 per cent of unfrozen food at any one time. If your freezer has a capacity of 100 litres (an average UK fridge-freezer), only stock it with up to 10 litres worth; this works out at about half a carrier bag's worth of shopping. If you're not sure how big your freezer is, simply search the model number online (usually on a sticker inside the door) and you should be able to get the answer pretty quickly!

Unless you have stacks of freezer space, if you want to keep a Freezer Stash of homemade 'ready-to-heat' meals, it's a safer option to simply double any meals that you cook fresh and freeze half for another day (more on this on the following pages).

. . . Leftovers

Ahhh, leftovers. Let's face it, we either love 'em or hate 'em.

I know many people swear by leftovers. They do, after all, make the perfect easy lunch or dinner. And if they work for you, that's brilliant. However, there are a huge number of people who are guilty of either:

A. Binning leftovers straightaway (maybe there's not 'enough' to make it worthwhile or you just don't fancy eating the same thing two days in a row).

B. Putting leftovers in a tub in the fridge and promptly forgetting about them, only to eventually throw them away a week or so later.

I most certainly used to fall into the second category. I had so many good intentions that went astray. In fact, about 25 per cent of the 4.7 million tonnes of food wasted in the UK every year is due to preparing, cooking and serving too much food.

What I've learnt about myself is that unless I'm definitely going to have leftovers for lunch the next day, the best thing I can do is freeze them. I'm not a fan of eating the same thing two days in a row, so by freezing the leftovers, they can become a meal for a future day when I really can't face cooking.

There are some useful things to note if you decide to start freezing your leftovers:

- **First of all, if you're guilty of having a lot of plate scrapings, start serving food to the middle of the table instead of served-up on plates.** That way everyone can take only what they want. Of course, kids are still likely to overload their plates, but at least the adults can be a bit more measured.

  You may even want to switch to using smaller plates, forcing everyone to take one serving and then consider whether they need another. Be wary of fast eaters (like my husband) though, who could easily clear the table before everyone else has drawn breath!

- **As I've mentioned previously, be sure to cool your leftovers and get them in the fridge or freezer within two hours (or one hour for rice).** Leftovers should be eaten within 48 hours (24 hours for rice), so you can technically freeze them up until this point too. I strongly recommend freezing them immediately though; it's safer, they'll better retain their quality and you won't end up kicking yourself days later when you realise that you forgot about the leftovers in the fridge and now they need to be binned.

- **If you can flat-freeze the leftovers (see page 72), then do so.** They'll take up less space in your freezer and you'll be able to defrost and reheat them much faster, so no need to defrost them in the fridge in advance.

- **Always freeze leftovers in usable portions – this might be a single portion, a double portion or a family-size portion.** You can only defrost and reheat the meal once, so you need to freeze in quantities that can be eaten in one go. Personally, I prefer single portions as they are faster to defrost and reheat, and they provide more flexibility.

- **Please, please, please *always* label your leftovers.** Relying on your memory to identify frozen meals will only result in a game of freezer roulette. I simply write on the top strip of the bag what it is, the number of portions and the date of freezing using a permanent marker (see page 64). There are freezer stickers that you can use, or freezer tape or good-quality masking tape can work well. There's always a risk of these falling off though, so writing directly on the bag is definitely my preferred option. The key is to label the bag before it is filled with food, and definitely before it goes in the freezer.

- **Make sure you reheat any leftovers *really* thoroughly, so they're piping hot throughout.** This is one scenario where having a food probe thermometer is super handy (see pages 60–1). I outline the required temperature and time combos on page 106.

- **If the quantity of leftovers is really too small to serve as a full meal, it doesn't mean they shouldn't be saved.** Small portions:

  - Make perfect quick and easy meals for kids

  - Are great for lunches, maybe served on a jacket potato or in a wrap

  - Can be bulked out to make a different dinner (this is where your Freezer Stash comes in). For example, a small portion of leftover chilli could be made into quesadillas or burritos using your Freezer Stash. Maybe you've got some surplus cooked rice, some guacamole, some black beans and grated cheese in the freezer? You've just got yourself a completely different and essentially free dinner.

Don't get too carried away when you make something new from your leftovers though, as you'll have reheated the food when you cooked your second meal. As they shouldn't be reheated more than once, leftovers of leftovers should be avoided at all costs!

If you're not sure about what leftovers you can freeze, there's a section that covers this under 'What the Heck Can You Freeze Anyway?' (see page 276), although this is in no way exhaustive.

If you have an aversion to batch cooking but find freezing leftovers works well for you, it's worth thinking about cooking 'intentional' leftovers; double the quantity of your recipe, so you can eat half straightaway and freeze half to eat later. Always remember to test freezing and reheating a small portion first though!

And remember 'leftovers' doesn't necessarily mean an entire cooked meal. They could be leftover cooked rice, leftover cooked pasta or leftover mashed potato, for example. Be sure to check out the 'What the Heck Can You Freeze Anyway?' section (see pages 270–92) for tips on freezing (and reheating) these!

. . . Meal Planning

If you're an avid meal planner, I take my hat off to you. Meal planning is something that I simply was not born to do. Whether you plan your full week (or month) or just a couple of days at a time, that's brilliant. But even if you are great at meal planning, inevitably there will still be occasions when your intentions are thwarted.

What I love is that you don't need to freeze everything all at once, you could just save the pepper that's looking a bit ropey or the chicken that needs using today. It might be that you keep to your original meal plan in terms of the recipe you cook, but using your now-frozen ingredients.

Try to use your newly acquired freezer knowledge pre-emptively. If you have a selection of meals that you always cook, why not prep some of the ingredients for a planned meal in advance? While your chilli is simmering on the hob, you could take two minutes to chop up and freeze the onions and peppers for the fajitas you've planned for later in the week.

This is particularly helpful if you've got one or two quieter days in the week when you can get ahead for busier days, and ensure that nothing goes off or gets used out of step with your plan.

. . . Winging It

Winging it is where I solidly belong. The truth be told, for me, this used to result in quite a lot of stress and a heavy reliance on 'popping to the shop' and convenience meals. If the freezer had run low on batch-cooked meals, I had nothing to bring to the table (quite literally).

The Full Freezer Method works perfectly for those inclined to wing it because everything is frozen with the end use in mind (see page 53 if you're not sure what I'm talking about!). Once you get your head around exactly what you can freeze and how, you're freed from the need to plan anything. You can defrost your food safely and quickly (see page 109) or cook it straight from frozen (see page 57).

As long as you keep your freezer full of ingredients that you like and freeze them in a way that makes them easy to use or quick to defrost, you can whip up a meal relatively quickly with minimal effort. And if your freezer starts to get too full, you can take a quick inventory (see page 33) and make a plan to use what you've got (saving you a trip to the shops and the additional cost).

. . . Allotments

If you've got an allotment, I'm assuming you must already be freezing at least some foods. When you have a glut, freezing is the obvious option. But you may not have realised that you can open-freeze your crops (see page 70) or that some bulky items can be cooked down and flat-frozen (see page 72).

For example, if you have huge crop of tomatoes and you know that they'll end up being cooked in a soup or stew, you could cook them down and flat-freeze them in usable portions (but keep in mind that if you do cook them, you'll be reheating them when you cook your soup or stew – see 'leftovers' on page 134 for more on this, as well as 'The Full Freezer Loop' on page 17).

If you have a glut of one particular food, to avoid waste, it may be best to share some of it. If your friends and family have had their fill of your homegrown courgettes and you're running out of ways to offload them, a simple box outside your home with a sign encouraging people to help themselves can work well, or use an app like Olio to pass them on to others.

. . . Fruit & Veg Boxes

Another group I have great admiration for are those who receive a regular fruit and vegetable delivery box . . . and actually *use the whole thing.*

I know some people plan their meals around the contents of their weekly box, which is a great idea and makes perfect sense. If you're like me though and never seem to be able to get through everything (especially if you aren't able to select what's in your box), it's useful to know that you can freeze the surplus. See the 'What the Heck Can You Freeze Anyway?' section on pages 252–270 to find out how you could be saving those precious fruit and veggies.

Try not to freeze any unfamiliar veggies just because you don't know whether they're something you'll like, or you're not sure how to cook them. If they go into your freezer, the chances of them never coming out are high!

You may need to reduce the frequency of your deliveries if you're now freezing foods that you would usually have binned. There are only so many carrots a person can eat! Fruit and veg boxes are such a great way to do your bit for the planet; whether they be local and seasonal, or misshapen that might have otherwise gone to waste. But you only get your eco-points if you eat everything!

. . . Meal Kit Deliveries

If you're anything like me, you'll love the idea of meal kit deliveries (such as HelloFresh, Gousto, Mindful Chef, etc), but in reality they may not work quite as you intended.

If you're not familiar with these types of kits, they're a really great idea for busy people who like variety and hate food waste. Basically, you select the meals that you like the look of and a box of ingredients turns up on your doorstep, ready for you to take on the mantel of culinary genius. They're a fantastic way to introduce variety into your mealtimes with minimal faff.

This plan can fall down because you have to decide what you want to eat *in advance*, which is much the same as meal planning . . . and you already know how I feel about that. Now, some people will be fine with this. After all, you can choose how many meals you want to be sent, so you don't *have* to eat from the meal kit box every night of the week for some flexibility. Of course, you might *love* that the meal kit makes those decisions for you. You can just cook and eat, job done.

Some of us, however, are fickle and as soon as the meal kit arrives, we want something else. Or it might simply be that your plans for the week have changed, or someone is sick and you end up not cooking.

Being able to press a pause button on some of the dishes that arrive in the meal kit to save them for another occasion is very useful. Just make sure you keep the ingredients grouped together in the freezer if you want to use them for the intended meal. Alternatively, if you no longer fancy the meal you picked, you can adjust what was planned by using your Freezer Stash. Match some of your fresh ingredients with foods from your freezer. This is particularly handy if you have unexpected guests and need to make your food stretch further.

It's also useful to remember that for some dishes, if the portion size cooked is more than you can manage, the excess can be frozen (read more about leftovers on page 276).

These meal kit boxes often end up getting cancelled because of the guilt that comes with regularly wasting one or two meals. But if you love them, make sure none of the meal kit food is wasted when plans change by using your freezer to ensure they keep on working well for you!

. . . Flavour Kits

What do I mean by 'flavour kits'? Well, these are generally seasonings that provide the flavour for your dish without including the main ingredients. You might have seen these in the supermarket (e.g. Schwartz, Maggi and Colman's), and you can even subscribe to delivery services such as Simply Cook which give you four meals (of your choice) in one box, posted through your front door as regularly as you like. Sauce kits such as Spice Tailor, Street Kitchen and Blue Dragon also fall into the 'flavour kits' category.

Because these kits don't include the main ingredients, it can be a bit frustrating if you need to pop to the shop to buy all of those ingredients fresh. If you have a Freezer Stash, however, life becomes far more flexible and convenient! With a selection of flavour kits in the cupboard and a stash of ready-to-use ingredients in the freezer, you can whip up a variety of meals in a jiffy!

TOP TIP

It's always worth checking out the website of your favourite flavour kit brand as they often have inspiration for different ways to use their products with various ingredients.

Unlike with portioned meal kits, you'll often end up with leftover main ingredients, but you can just prep and freeze these while you're cooking, so you have them ready to use for another meal on another day (check 'What the Heck Can You Freeze Anyway?' on page 197 to see just how much you could be freezing).

. . . Fakeaways

I won't lie. I love a takeaway. Not having to prepare the food or do any washing up massively appeals to me, but I *cannot* eat takeaway food every day and nor would I want to.

If you find yourself relying on takeaways because you're too busy to plan, prep and cook, I totally get it. And it might be that you're simply in a phase of your life when you need some convenient options. However, it's well worth considering whether a Freezer Stash could help you cook from scratch faster and more easily, saving you a substantial amount of cash. After all, it's estimated the average Brit spends over £600 a year on takeaways!

To get you started, there are stacks of ready-prepped frozen products, such as stir-fry mixes, which are healthy, quick and affordable. And of course, because they're frozen, they won't go off, so you have the flexibility to use them as and when you need them.

With help from flavour kits, ready-frozen produce and foods you've prepped and frozen yourself (as and when you can), it's possible to throw together quick meals faster than a takeaway can be delivered.

I know this might be a bit of a tricky habit to break, particularly if you have a significant other who is always turning to delivery apps. Remember, this isn't about ditching takeaways altogether, unless you want to!

To help you get started, jot down some of your favourite dishes opposite and consider whether these could be switched for a 'fakeaway' instead. If you're unsure, look online at the freezer and cupboard sections of a supermarket's website. If you've got the time and inclination, you could scratch-cook your favourite takeaway dish (e.g. make your own burgers), but there's nothing wrong with having some 'sling-in-the oven' foods in your Freezer Stash if they help you resist the takeaway.

If you're not ready to ditch takeaways altogether, could you cut down your order by making some of it at home? For example, heating frozen ready-made bhajis in the air fryer or reheating some frozen cooked rice (perfect for egg-fried rice, you can even chuck in some frozen peas!).

My favourite takeaway dishes	What can I easily make instead?
1.	1.
2.	2.
3	3
4.	4.
5.	5.

. . . Healthy Eating

There are a few ways in which having a Freezer Stash can help you eat more healthily:

- **Eat more fruit and veg (without any waste)** I used to struggle to see how I could get a variety of fruit and veggies into my diet, because I'd buy stuff and it would go off before I could get through all of it. Knowing that I can press a pause button on my fruit and veggies means I now buy far more, more frequently. There's never any need for fresh produce to go in the bin, or feel like my money is being wasted.

  Also, because the fruit and veggies are there (and I don't even need to defrost them), I have no excuse not to use them. I can grab a variety of different fruits and whip up a smoothie or cook up some veggies in very little time at all.

- **Cut down on takeaways and convenience foods** As discussed on pages 145–7, if there's a Freezer Stash of healthy ingredients available to us, it's far easier to resist the lure of takeaways or relying on convenience foods!

- **Eat more moderate sized portions** So many of us are guilty of overloading our plates when we cook too much food, then forcing ourselves to eat it just to avoid any waste. Those excessive portions are often a result of using up ingredients just because they need to be used, when in reality you can use part of an ingredient and freeze the rest (or cook using ready-prepped frozen ingredients). Even if you do accidentally cook too much, your freezer can be used to save the excess for another day.

. . . Variety

I know I've covered this already in relation to meal and flavour kits, but I honestly cannot emphasise this enough!

I'm the cook in our family and one of the things my husband loves most about me developing The Full Freezer Method is the huge variety of meals we now enjoy. We rarely eat the same dish more than once a month (if that).

Not only does my Freezer Stash work perfectly with the meal and flavour kits mentioned previously, but I actually have the headspace to be more creative. That's not to say that I'm the most adventurous of cooks, but I now have the bandwidth to think how meals can be tweaked to avoid dinnertimes getting boring (see pages 165–8 for my secret!).

. . . Being On a Budget

When you're strapped for cash, the advice is often to batch cook or plan meals so that you can make the most of the ingredients you have. For example, roasting a whole chicken on a Sunday (which is cheaper than buying individual cuts) means you can use the meat for more meals over the following days (up to 48 hours from the fridge or a lot longer from the freezer). This is great advice. And if you're conscious of your energy usage too, this will likely be the most cost-efficient option.

It's still handy to know that you can press a pause button on individual ingredients too, so you can avoid wasting anything ever again. This affords you some variety within your meals (instead of having to eat the same food three days in a row) and also enables you to stretch particular ingredients so you can make smaller portions of more meals and take advantage of discounts, bulk buying or yellow-sticker offers.

. . . Babies

Now, I'm not going to claim to be any sort of expert when it comes to weaning. I have two young kids, so I've been through the process, but I'll be honest, those years are mostly a sleep-deprived blur!

What I *am* confident of is how I would have really benefited from developing The Full Freezer Method *before* I weaned my kids.

I did use my freezer to some degree. With my eldest, I made purées and mini batch-cooked meals to feed her (as well as most of the other kids in my NCT group). I also did 'freezer meal swaps' with some friends; we would each cook one thing, keep some for ourselves and then swap small quantities of the rest so that we all had greater variety. The freezer was also useful for homemade snacks, like low-sugar and savoury muffins and pancakes.

What I didn't realise was that I could freeze individual pieces of vegetables (see 'What the Heck Can You Freeze Anyway?' on page 262). When a weaning book encouraged me to give my daughter a different vegetable every day, I would feel totally overwhelmed.

I know the obvious thing is to eat the rest of the vegetables yourself, but in those days, I don't think I was doing a huge amount of daily cooking. I was relying on my batch-cooked meals, shop-bought convenience foods, takeaways and, if I'm totally honest, an excessive number of biscuits.

When the penny dropped that I could prep and freeze vegetables, such as broccoli and cauliflower florets, courgette and carrot batons and sweet potato chips, I was kicking myself. I could have literally cooked just one or two pieces at a time.

And for those foods served uncooked, such as

avocado, banana and tomatoes, I could have given it to my kids fresh, then frozen the surplus to use in baking and cooked dishes.

If I had understood 'The Full Freezer Loop' (see page 17) too, I could have really reduced our food waste as well; knowing that it's okay to freeze raw or blanched veggies, cook with them at a later date, freeze some portions of that dish and reheat it once.

IMPORTANT: BABY FOOD

If you're prepping and freezing food for your child, make sure it cools quickly (see page 101), and when you reheat it, follow the recommended time and temperature combinations on page 106. You must not just 'warm' the food; it needs to be reheated until piping hot and then allowed to cool to a safe feeding temperature.

If you're rolling your eyes at me for being quite so 'homely' with my first child, I'm not at all ashamed to admit that I relied on shop-bought foods far more with the second one. I was, quite frankly, too sleep-deprived and emotionally frayed to spend my time puréeing carrots only to have them hurled on the floor. .

We did quickly feel the financial implications of relying on shop-bought foods though, especially as our son would only eat such small amounts. Anything that hadn't been touched would go in the fridge, but it would usually still end up being wasted as I would forget it was there (or he refused it and I couldn't face having the same food thrown at me two days in a row).

It never occurred to me that I might be able to freeze some of these shop-bought foods (I know right, proper lightbulb moment!). I could have easily halved a ready meal and frozen it before heating, then only heated and served each half at a time. And I could have frozen fruit and veg purées in ice-cube trays.

Unfortunately, I can't give you an overview of what you can and can't freeze in terms of shop-bought baby foods – there are simply too many brands and their manufacturing processes could change at any time. But I thoroughly encourage you to stop and think before you put that jar or pouch in the bin. Could it be frozen instead? If you think it might be a good candidate for freezing, contact the manufacturer (there are usually contact details on the packaging or online) to check if there are any food safety reasons why something can't be frozen. A lot of food manufacturers will say not to freeze as it can affect the quality, but that doesn't mean it's not safe to try!

IMPORTANT: CONTAMINATION

You should never freeze foods that have been partially eaten, such as a pouch that a child has already sucked from or food from their plate. Only freeze untouched foods!

. . . Little Kids

Pretty much every parent will have had the go-to kids' foods in the freezer at some point. Chicken nuggets, fish fingers, peas . . . they're a given, right? And I don't have a problem with any of them.

What I love about my Freezer Stash is that I can also have home-prepped sweet potato wedges, carrot batons for roasting, broccoli florets for steaming and a whole stash of fruit for smoothies.

I'm not saying my kids always eat the veggies, but being able to have a couple of bits on the table (even when the kids are eating separately from us), means they're at least being exposed to the good stuff and have the opportunity to try it. This massively helps to ease my mum-guilt when they've had cheese sandwiches for lunch every single day (and minimises the amount of veg ending up in the bin).

We're still working on increasing the variety of fruit and vegetables they eat, but it's definitely much easier knowing that we have lots of different things in stock and we can freeze any surplus ingredients if we can't get through them fast enough.

I've also found getting the kids to help with washing and prepping fruit and veg for the freezer is a really nice way to introduce different fresh produce without any pressure to eat them. Granted, as someone who likes things 'just so', seeing the way my children peel and chop veggies (with kid-safe tools available via my Amazon shop – www.amazon.co.uk/shop/thefullfreezer) is pretty hard, but I know they're great skills for them to learn for the future!

. . . Big Kids

The age at which your kids start cooking independently is going to vary from child to child. Within my own family, we've had a normally sensible teen putting a knife in the toaster and another trying to melt chocolate on the hob in a Pyrex dish (with no pan of water). Not all young adults can be trusted alone in the kitchen.

Getting kids into the habit of saving foods by freezing them and ensuring that they understand how to keep their food safe is invaluable, whatever age they are and however capable they are in the kitchen.

They can start quite young, helping out with prepping food for the freezer, so even if you're nervous about letting them loose near a frying pan or hot oven, they can still feel part of the cooking process.

If you're keen to get your kids cooking, then having a Freezer Stash of ingredients ready for them to use (under supervision until you *know* they're capable) is incredibly useful, and so much less stressful than doing everything from scratch. Even just being able to make a smoothie or reheat some pancakes can be handy skills to have when they're peckish. And as they get older and start to become independent, the benefits are two-fold:

1. **Ever bought food for dinner only for your child to tell you at the last minute that they're going out?** No worries. If you've started cooking, you know how to freeze the leftovers. And if you haven't, you know how you can freeze and save the ingredients if you need to.

2. **Ever cooked your child dinner only for them to state that they're 'still hungry' and they essentially want another dinner?** Excellent, they can use the bits and pieces in the freezer to make themselves an omelette, pizza or a pasta dish (whether or not they find this acceptable is out of your control, but the option is there if you can work with them to ensure there's stuff in the freezer that they like!).

And if your kid is heading off to university or moving into their own place, getting them set up with a freezer full of food (whether it's a Freezer Stash or batch-cooked meals) is nicely reassuring.

Depending on how far away they are, and how concerned you are about them consuming some proper food, you could also cook intentional leftovers at home and build up a variety of different meals for them to reheat. You would need to make sure you pack them following the advice on page 44, to ensure they stay frozen on the journey!

. . . An Empty Nest

I hate this term, so I apologise for using it, but it's the best way to describe this phase of life. The kids are all grown up and off they go out into the big wide world.

There will be some easy adjustments, such as no longer buying foods that only the kids ate. However, when it comes to cooking, it can be difficult to gauge the portion sizes for yourself (and perhaps a partner), when you were previously cooking for growing adults as well.

Now that you know how to freeze your leftovers (see page 134), these foods at least won't go to waste. Even carbs like pasta, rice (see page 292) and mashed potato (see page 270) can be frozen and saved for another meal.

Building up your Freezer Stash of ingredients can also be helpful as you figure out the 'new normal' for this phase of your life. You don't need to use a whole onion just because it's there, you can use half and freeze half. And when you have that stash of frozen ingredients there and ready to go, you can alter your portion sizes to suit your appetite.

It's also super handy when the kids decide to 'pop

in' for a surprise visit. If you've got a well-stocked freezer, you already have a meal good to go without too much faff!

. . . Single Life

If you live alone, cooking can be such a frustrating task. When I lived by myself, I would often end up having a bowl of cereal or a piece of toast. I hated having to strategize to avoid waste, then if my plans changed, any leftovers (meals or ingredients) would end up in the bin. It also drove me crazy that some shops would only sell multipacks of fresh ingredients – there are only so many potatoes one person can eat!

Knowing how to prep and freeze practically everything means you can buy that multipack without any resentment, and your food can easily last for weeks or even months.

Having ingredients ready-prepped for those nights when you really can't face cooking is super helpful. Even if you just chuck together a simple pizza or omelette, it's *way* more satisfying than yet another bowl of cereal.

And if you find most recipes are for four people or more, you can divide the ingredients by the number of portions and cook for one. If doing this means you only need a quarter of an onion, that's fine – you can freeze the rest (or just use a quarter of an onion from your Freezer Stash)!

And if you want to cook for two and freeze those leftover portions for another day, that's an option too (see page 134 for my top tips on this!).

. . . Difficult Times

As I mentioned at the beginning of this book, ill health was the catalyst that sparked my love for my freezer.

If you experience poor health, or a loved one is unwell, or if you're bereaved, going through separation, divorce, or financial difficulties, knowing how to use your freezer more effectively *may* help to ease the burden. It clearly cannot relieve grief or stress, but knowing that you have food in stock and are able to stretch food further can provide some comfort.

Using your freezer more effectively means you can:

- **Prepare foods when you feel well, so that you have something for the bad days**

- **Have a Freezer Stash of ingredients, so it's much easier to prepare a meal for one**

- **Have a Freezer Stash of ingredients, so it's much easier to prepare smaller portions or something**

plain for someone who is unwell and hasn't got much appetite (and you may be able to freeze leftovers if they can't face eating; remember not to overload their plate if this is likely, so only serve small amounts and then offer more if required)

- **Freeze leftovers if you accidentally cook too much**

- **Stretch ingredients further and avoid any waste**

If you're witnessing a friend or family member going through any of these challenges, getting their freezer in order and ensuring they have food available to them is a great way to support them and show you care.

. . . Holidays

I know you're going to hate me a little bit for adding *another* thing to your holiday to-do list, but this one is well worth it.

In those final days before going on holiday, you might be in a habit of 'running down' the fridge and using everything up. If so, that's great. But if you're guilty of hurriedly chucking the contents of your fridge into a bin liner just before you leave the house or coming home to a fridge full of slightly fuzzy food, this one is for you . . .

By adding 'freeze the contents of the fridge' to your holiday to-do list, not only do you avoid any waste, but you also have that food to eat on your return! I find flat-freezing milk in bags in usable portions particularly handy (see page 234 for more on freezing milk). The milk can be defrosted quickly in a dish of cold water, ready for a cup of tea or bowl of porridge. Having meat and veggies in the freezer is also super useful for whipping up a quick dinner.

Alleviating the guilt around binning perfectly good food feels great, and then benefitting from your organisation after a long journey home feels even better!

. . . Christmas & Other Celebrations

I'm focusing here on Christmas because it's a big thing in our family, but using your freezer to prep ahead for any celebration is a great way to reduce stress and allows you to enjoy the day. When it comes to Christmas, pretty much everything can be prepared in advance, and doesn't even need to be fully cooked before freezing. For example, you only need to blanch or parboil your veggies and then they can be cooked straight from frozen on the big day.

Remember, if you're preparing cooked dishes in advance and reheating them for your celebration, the food can only be reheated once.

In the 'What the Heck Can You Freeze Anyway?' section

(see page 197), you can find guidance for potatoes, parsnips, carrots, sprouts, pigs in blankets, gravy and much more.

The many joys of prepping ahead are:

1. **You can prep in stages whenever you have the time**

2. **You can spread the cost over a longer period**

3. **You can share the load** (you could prep for someone else to help them, or someone else could help you prep)

4. **You don't need to worry about the shops running out of anything –** you can relax knowing you've got everyone's favourites well in advance

5. **You can cook only as much as you need on the day**

6. **You can freeze everything in usable portions** (e.g. stuffing, bread sauce, cranberry sauce) so you only use as much as you need

7. **You can make the leftovers into another meal because they've only been cooked once,** but keep in mind that whatever you make (e.g. turkey curry!) should not be frozen as you'll have already reheated the leftovers when you cooked the second meal. If you prefer to cook with your leftovers at a later date, you're better to open-freeze the leftovers.

The greatest joy is being able to spend more time with your friends and family, instead of being stuck in a hot kitchen and then overwhelmed with stacks of washing up. Of course, if you want to skip to the good bit, there's no judgement from me if you choose to buy everything pre-prepped and frozen from the supermarket. As I mentioned previously, there are even cook-from-frozen joints (see page 120) available now, so you may not even need to defrost the turkey!

Why Your Freezer is For Life

It's important to remember that our priorities change throughout life – what works for you now might change later on. Clearly you're interested in making better use of your freezer, otherwise you wouldn't be reading this book, but it's worth keeping in mind that how you use your freezer is likely to change over the years.

It might be that you're currently in the batch cooking camp and continue to prep like this (while freezing those little bits and bobs) because having ready-to-heat meals is more valuable to you at the moment than having total flexibility and variety.

Or you may only have a small freezer now, but as you become more comfortable with freezing and as your life changes (moving house, for example), you may decide to invest in more freezer space.

The most important thing is to find what works best for you and to know that your freezer can help you out, however you choose to cook.

Ditch the Dinnertime Rut

We all get stuck in a bit of a rut with mealtimes. It's understandable given the number of decisions we have to make in a single day. By the time dinnertime rolls around, our brains are usually fried.

In order to 'mix up' mealtimes, you need the mental space to find new recipes, go shopping for ingredients and then actually cook the darn thing. It can be pretty overwhelming and it ends up being easier to make the same things on repeat, even though you're bored of them.

If you want a shortcut, the meal and flavour kits discussed earlier (see pages 142 and 144) are a great starting point.

Alternatively, a simple way to find endless inspiration is to start with what you know and then tweak things. This is a technique I learnt from a great couple, DaChi (David and Chido Plunkett), who have been working in the catering industry for years and now run their own private dining company.

In the space below, write down all of the dishes that you know you can make (either off the top of your head or with a quick look at a recipe).

....

....

....

....

On each line below, list the same dishes you wrote above and note down the different carbs you could serve alongside each meal. Could you serve it with rice, pasta, noodles, potato, sweet potato, tortilla wraps, tortilla chips, slices of bread or something else?

....

....

....

....

Think about the flavours of each dish. Is there any way you could alter the dishes by adding different herbs or spices? For example, give tomato pasta a twist with some paprika or chilli. If you're not sure where to start with this, the internet is your friend! Simply search for your dish and add 'with a twist' (e.g. macaroni cheese with a twist). Jot down any recipe ideas that you'd like to try below.

....

....

....

....

Finally, consider the protein in the dishes – could you switch chicken for pork or beef? If you're veggie or vegan, think about whether the veg, pulses, nuts etc. in the dish could be switched up to create different combinations. Jot down your ideas below.

....

....

....

....

You should now have a whole raft of tweaks to your original list of recipes which could make your mealtimes more interesting without too much effort! Pick out three that you're going to cook soon and pop a sticky note on your fridge to remind you. Bonus points if you already have all the ingredients in your Freezer Stash!

TOP TIP

If you need inspiration for using up your stocks (both fresh and frozen), there are online resources you can turn to. I like to use a brilliant website and app called Supercook. You simply input your ingredients and it gives you a selection of recipes that you can make from them!

PHASE 5:
Don't Freeze Up

I'm hoping by now you're feeling pretty buzzed. You might be questioning if it's normal to be this excited about your freezer. If so, you've just joined a rapidly growing family of Freezer Geeks. Welcome!

I'm so pleased that you're a convert to using the freezer and now understand how it can make your life easier. Yes, people will think you're weird for finding your freezer so thrilling, but that's just because they don't understand yet.

I pass the baton on to you now to spread the message of just how helpful a freezer can be. And if you're not sure you can convince others, this book makes a great birthday gift/Mother's day gift/Father's day gift/ housewarming gift (delete as applicable). Keep talking to them about it – they will thank you in the long run!

If you're not yet convinced by The Full Freezer Method, it may be that something is holding you back. There are a few common stumbling blocks that tend to crop up when I'm talking to people about freezing, so I want to address those here. If you can't spot your particular hurdle, reach out to me via social media (@TheFullFreezer) to see if I can help you hop over it. It might just be that the time isn't right or that it's not your cup of tea after all, but if you've come up against a barrier, I want to help you get past it.

1. I have a small freezer

This is everyone's first obstacle. Yes, of course, if you have limited freezer space, it's difficult to freeze lots of stuff. I'm not demanding that you freeze *everything* though. What I want is for you to know that you *can* freeze certain foods and that you *can* use your freezer more effectively.

Although you have a small freezer now and are limited in how much you can freeze, it doesn't mean that you won't move somewhere with a bigger freezer in the future. The knowledge you hold now may sway your decisions around the importance of having freezer space, or it might be that you use this information to help parents, siblings or friends to better utilise their space.

In the meantime, the best thing you can do is decide

what's most important to you. It might be that you want to prioritise freezing flavour boosts, such as chilli, herbs, garlic or ginger. It could be that you want to make any meat purchases as cost-effective as possible by bulk buying and then portion up the meat to save space. If you're on a health kick, it could be that fruit and veggies are the priority, or you might just want to do what you can to reduce your food waste and your freezer space is used as a pause button to gain a couple of days here and there.

The most crucial thing to remember is that your freezer isn't only for long-term storage and that if you freeze food using the techniques on pages 70–85 and keep the end use in mind (see page 53), you'll likely be far better off than you are now.

2. I struggle to find the time to freeze food (then I feel guilty because I know I *could* have frozen it)

First things first, don't beat yourself up. For some people, this process can take time to adjust to. You're most likely working against decades of daily habits and putting new routines in place doesn't happen overnight.

Start by trying to save easy things – items you can literally bung in the freezer in a freezer bag (e.g. garlic) or that you can quickly chop up and freeze (e.g. peppers or spring onions). Or prepare extra of an ingredient and freeze the excess (e.g. roast potatoes). Do what you can for now, and celebrate the wins. It's better to make small, gradual steps forward rather than write off the idea altogether!

3. I organised my freezer, but it's a mess again

I'm going to let you in on a little secret. My freezer is not 100 per cent organised all of the time. There are times when shopping arrives and I just stuff shop-bought frozen food into the freezer (although I do my best to at least put things in the right place, space-allowing!).

Because I have a system and because each space in my freezer is labelled, it's quick and easy for me to rectify the situation and get things back in order. The whole point of The Full Freezer Method is that it's flexible and that it's about progress, not perfection.

If you find yourself in a bit of a muddle, simply revisit the 'The 5C Freezer Clear Down' (see page 27). You should only need to redo steps one, two and five, so the time required will be minimal. Going through this process usually ends up saving you time and money as you can probably take some things off your shopping list!

If you know you're likely to let things slip completely, it can be useful to add a regular reminder to quickly organise the freezer to the calendar on your phone.

Aim for once a month, but if you only have a smaller freezer it may need to be weekly. Pair sorting your freezer with something you enjoy doing – listen to a podcast, audiobook or your favourite album and challenge yourself to get the job done before your episode ends.

4. I'm terrified my freezer will malfunction and I'll lose all my food

This is a totally valid concern, but remember, a lot of the food you're likely to have frozen would previously have ended up in the bin anyway! That's not to say it wouldn't still be gutting given that you have taken the time to save it (and of course, you may have purposefully built a Freezer Stash of useful ingredients), but at least you'll have tried to save the food instead of binning it.

In the case of an actual freezer emergency, all is not lost if you have a Freezer Stash of ingredients rather than cooked meals. You can still take action to save at least some of your food!

Scenario 1: Power Cut

- **DO NOT open the door** If you keep the door shut, a full freezer should maintain its temperature for at least 48 hours, or 24 hours if it's half full.

- **Monitor the temperature** I recommend investing in a freezer thermometer with an external display so that you can monitor the temperature without opening the door. Your freezer might also have a light on the outside to indicate if it gets too warm (check the user manual if this isn't obvious).

- **Relocate food using coolers** If you know someone whose freezer is not affected, see if you can relocate some of your food (remember to mark what's yours with a permanent marker).

- **Save what you can and keep a record** If your power cut lasts a while and you're not sure if the food is still safe, apply the tips in Scenario 2 before binning anything. Remember to take photos of anything that you throw away as you may be able to claim on your insurance (you might already have these photos if you've done a freezer inventory, but it's good to be certain of what you're actually having to chuck out).

Scenario 2: Door Left Open

- **Check the food** Any items that usually require refrigeration or freezing that have fully thawed and are now warm should be thrown away. This particularly applies to ice cream, which should never be thawed and refrozen for safety reasons.

- **Save what you can** Any items that are still frozen (with ice crystals present) can stay in the freezer. Simply shut the door and leave it closed to help it return to the correct temperature faster. If you have a fast-freeze setting, turn this on.

- **Consider cooking** Any thawed, uncooked foods that are still cold (under 8°C) can be moved to the fridge and cooked within 24 hours. You then have up to 48 hours to eat or freeze what you've cooked. Any ready-to-eat items that have defrosted and are still cold (under 8°C) should be refrigerated and eaten within 24 hours.

- **Give away the surplus** Instead of binning perfectly good food, offer it to friends and family (or invite them over!). You can also offer the food to strangers via the free app Olio or www.freemymeal.co.uk.

5. How do I adapt a recipe to cook just a single portion using my Freezer Stash?

If you have a recipe for four people but you want to cook for one, simply divide the ingredients by four. If you search online for 'recipe converter calculator' you'll find websites which allow you to enter the web address for your recipe, amend the number of servings you want to cook and the calculator will do the sums for you.

INSURANCE

Most insurance companies will not cover the general wear and tear of your freezer itself, but your home insurance will often cover the contents under circumstances such as power outages. You're unlikely to be covered if the power has been accidentally turned off, if the power outage was planned or if the freezer is over 10 years old, and you can't claim for foods that haven't spoilt.

You'll need a list and photos of the foods that have spoilt, and of course, you'll have to weigh up whether it's worth claiming (the average freezer contents value is around £300, but yours may be worth more if you've been freezing everything!).

If your freezer is going to be filled up with particularly high-cost foods (for example, shop-bought prepped foods for Christmas or a celebration such as a wedding) you may also want to check if your insurer offers 'Celebration Cover'.

Most savoury recipes don't need to be exact either, so if you need a quarter of an onion, it's okay for you to guess the amount (after all, onions come in a range of sizes!).

It may be that the cooking times can be reduced too, so it's important to keep an eye on your food and use your food probe thermometer (see pages 60–1) to check your dish is a safe temperature even if it appears to be ready.

6. Even though I've built a Freezer Stash, I still find that I'm sometimes missing ingredients that I need.

The beauty of cooking is that it's as much an art as it is a science. With the internet now at our fingertips, it's easy to find substitutions for ingredients that we don't have. For example, onions might be used instead of leeks, and Greek yoghurt or sour cream could substitute crème fraîche.

Simply type 'what can I use instead of [insert ingredient here]' into a search engine and you'll get all sorts of inspiration!

7. I've read the food safety commandments (see page 101), but I still have food safety worries . . .

If you're still nervous about freezing, you can grab a copy of my *Freezer Geek's Guide to Food Safety* for free at

www.thefullfreezer.com/safety. In this guide, I provide
a downloadable cheat sheet which provides a simple
summary of all you need to know, alongside further detail
for those wanting to understand the 'why'. Also, follow
@FoodSafetyMum who provides loads of useful tips.

One Hurdle That Can't Be Overcome (Sorry!)

As I mentioned on pages 59–60, the one absolute
necessity if you're going to start home freezing is that
your freezer is cold enough to do the job properly. If your
freezer doesn't have a four-star rating, it should only be
used in the following ways:

3-Star = -18°C – storing shop-bought frozen food for up to 3 months

2-Star = -12°C – storing shop-bought frozen food for 15–20 days

1-Star = -6°C – storing shop-bought frozen food for 3–4 days

If your freezer is 4-Star rated (-18°C or colder) but your
freezer thermometer says it's not this cold, try the
following tech checks.

Tech Checks (Helping Your Freezer Run Efficiently)

It's really easy to neglect our freezers, but making sure they're properly looked after can help to ensure they run efficiently, they freeze our food safely and they cost less money to run. Here are a few things you can be doing to keep your freezer in good working order:

- **Get yourself a fridge and freezer thermometer** Even if your fridge and freezer have an in-built thermometer, having an external display with remote sensors will allow you to monitor the temperature throughout your appliance (without opening the door) and get a clear picture of whether the unit is actually working properly.

- **Clean the condenser coils at the back of the appliance** Unplug the freezer and use a soft brush and vacuum cleaner to clear any dust from the coils. If it's not obvious how to access these, check the user manual for your appliance for guidance. This job should only need to be done once or twice a year.

- **Check the door seal** This should be cleaned regularly, and if any cracks are found it'll need to be replaced.

A simple test to check if your door seal is working effectively is to close a piece of paper in the door and see if it's held in place. If the paper falls or can be easily pulled out then your seal may need replacing. If it's not cracked, try tightening up the hinges as this can help to fix the seal.

- **Don't crowd your appliance** Freezers (and fridges) need air to circulate not just inside them, but also around them in order to work effectively. Your freezer should have at least 5cm of clear space on each side, be installed away from ovens and radiators and ideally kept out of direct sunlight.

When using your freezer, there are also steps that you can take to help it not have to work so hard:

- **Don't leave the door open longer than necessary** By organising your fridge as shown on page 191, and your freezer following the steps in this book, you won't need to spend so long searching for your food – you should be able to grab it and get the door closed pretty much immediately.

- **Don't put hot or warm food in your fridge or freezer** Doing this will raise the temperature in the appliance and make it have to work harder. Plus, it puts your food at risk of harmful bacteria developing (see page 102).

- **If possible, keep your freezer around 75 per cent full** This is because the cold food will stop as much warm air rushing in. If you need to, you can use bottles and containers filled with water to take up empty space, but don't pack the space so much that you can't find things and have to leave the door open for longer!

I know it can be super tempting to read through this advice and not take action, so I've designated the next page for jotting down at least three changes you plan to make.

Do you need to buy a fridge/freezer thermometer and check the temperature? Do you need to stop overcrowding your appliance? Maybe you need to change the way you store some foods? Or stop putting hot food in the fridge? Remember to tell anyone else that uses your fridge or freezer too!

I PROMISE I WON'T FORGET TO . . .

1. _____

2. _____

3. _____

What If Your Freezer is on its Last Legs?

Okay, I want to stress that I'm *not* telling you to go out and buy a new freezer. Minimising our impact on the environment is one of the fundamental purposes of The Full Freezer Method, so if we all cast out our existing tech and buy a shiny new freezer, we won't be doing our best for the planet.

However, it may well be that your existing freezer is no longer up to the job and cannot be fixed (it's always worth getting a freezer engineer out to check first), and in this case, there are a few things worth considering:

1. **Where is your freezer going to live?** It's important to understand how freezers are affected by the

temperature surrounding them, so if it's too cold (or hot), they can stop working. If you'll be keeping your freezer in an outbuilding, make sure it has the right technical specification for this space and be sure to follow the appliance instructions when installing it. It might be boring, but it's worth taking those extra few minutes to make sure your freezer won't unexpectedly pack-in!

2. **Chest freezer or upright?** If you have a big family or grow your own produce, a chest freezer might be exactly what you need. Because they don't have structured shelves you can pack a lot more in and fit larger irregular shapes, such as joints of meat. Because of this lack of structure, it's also a lot easier to lose your food (particularly if you're short and can't easily reach the bottom!). A lot of people buy a chest freezer simply because it's what their parents had, but they're rarely a practical solution! Personally, if I had the floor space for a chest freezer (along with the need for that much freezer space and the budget allowed!), I would opt for two tall freezers. Despite the higher upfront cost and the ongoing running costs, I know that I would use a tall freezer far more effectively as I would be able to access the contents more easily.

3. **Is the model frost-free?** Lots of models these days have frost-free technology, which means you never need to defrost them. A feature well worth having!

4. **How energy efficient is it?** This can be fairly disheartening when you're shopping for a freezer, as at the time of writing this book, most freezers are classified as 'E' or 'F' in terms of energy efficiency – sounds pretty awful when 'A' is the gold standard, right? The reason for this is that the energy-efficiency rating system was changed in March 2021 (you might recall there used to be confusing A+, A++ and A+++ ratings). The new rating system works on a simple A–F rating, where 'A' is the most efficient. The key thing to remember when buying a new freezer is to go for the most energy-efficient model that you can afford, as the ongoing running cost of this will be lower. A more efficient model could save you as much as £100 per year, so considering your appliance should last between 11–20 years, it's worth spending a little more upfront, if you can.

5. **Does it have a space for open- and flat-freezing?** Some freezers include a tray (which often ends up being used for ice cubes), where you can easily open- and flat-freeze foods. Having an open shelf also makes it easier to freeze foods in this way. You

can still open- and flat-freeze foods in drawer space
or chest freezer, you just need to ensure that the tray
you use has sides so nothing falls off and becomes
buried. If you're in the market for a new fridge,
consider one with a decent 4-star-rated ice box, so
you can use that space to open- and flat-freeze
foods and then move them to your main freezer once
frozen solid.

IMPORTANT: WARRANTY

Always register your freezer if it has a warranty.
This usually only takes a few minutes, but could save
you a serious headache if it malfunctions

Making Foods Last Longer
(Without the Freezer)

Obviously, I'm a hardcore freezer advocate, but even I know that freezing *everything* isn't always possible or practical. My main objective is for you to have more delicious food that lasts you longer, so I want to include a section on things you can do to make your food last longer *before* it hits the freezer.

Know Your Onions
(When it Comes to Food Storage)

Did you know that certain foods can make other foods go off faster? Storing your foods incorrectly can lead to some fresh produce ripening and rotting more quickly.

- **Potatoes and onions should be stored separately as the levels of moisture in both causes the other to go off faster.** Ideally, you should keep your onions in a cool dark cupboard inside a breathable bag, whilst potatoes can go in the fridge* or in a separate cool dark cupboard.

- **To make salad leaves last longer, place a sheet of kitchen paper in the tub or bag to absorb moisture, then change this sheet every day or so.**

- **Store vegetables such as broccoli and celery in a jug of water (make sure you trim the stalks and change the water every day or two).** You can also revive sad-looking vegetables such as carrots by trimming off the ends and submerging them in cold water for a few hours!

- **Fruit such as bananas and apples emit ethylene gases as they ripen, so it's a good idea to keep them away from ethylene sensitive fruit and vegetables.** The table on page 189 provides an overview of which fruit and vegetables give off ethylene and which are sensitive to it. Just to really keep us on our toes, it's possible for fruit and veg to emit the gas *and* be sensitive to it. One very useful product is 'Fruit and Veg Saver Bags' which absorb ethylene gas. Simply wrap your different fruits and veggies in separate bags and your fresh produce could last up to two or three times longer. These bags can be washed and reused, but if you would prefer to avoid using plastic, storing your fruit and vegetables in separate glass containers can help too. It's also important to keep an eye on your fruit and move any very ripe pieces away from your other produce. The saying 'one bad apple can spoil the barrel' is spot on – the riper a fruit is, the more ethylene it produces and the faster everything around it will ripen and then rot. It's worth noting that cut flowers give off ethylene too, so never display them next to your fruit bowl if you want your fruit to last.

*The Food Standards Agency used to advise against keeping potatoes in the fridge due to concerns about acrylamide which has links with cancer, but this guidance was removed in March 2023.

Emits Ethylene Gas		Sensitive to Ethylene Gas	
FRUIT	**VEG**	**FRUIT**	**VEG**
Apples	Asparagus	Apples	Cucumbers
Apricots	Aubergines	Apricots	Okra
Avocados	Beans, green	Avocados	
Bananas	Broccoli	Bananas	
Currants,	Brussels sprouts	Blackberries	
red/black	Cabbage	Blood oranges	
Gooseberries	Carrots	Blueberries	
Grapefruit	Cauliflower	Cantaloupe	
Grapes	Celery	melons	
Guavas	Chillies	Cherries, sweet	
Kiwifruit	Cucumbers	Currants,	
Lemons	Greens,	red/black	
Limes	spring	Figs, fresh	
Mandarins /	Herbs, fresh	Gooseberries	
Tangerines	Kale	Grapefruit	
Mangoes	Leeks	Grapes	
Melons,	Lettuce, Iceberg,	Guavas	
Cantaloupe or	Cos or Romaine	Honeydew	
Honeydew	Okra	melons	
Nectarines	Mangetout	Kiwifruit	
Oranges	Pak choi	Lemons	
Papayas	Parsnips	Limes	
Passion fruit	Potatoes	Lychees	
Peaches	Pumpkins	Mandarins /	
Pears	Radicchio	Tangerines	
Persimmons	Radishes	Mangoes	
Plantains	Salad leaves	Melons	
Plums	Shallots	Nectarines	
Quinces	Spinach	Oranges	
Tomatoes	Spring onions	Papayas	
Watermelons	Squash	Passion fruit	
	Sweet potatoes	Peaches	
	Turnips	Pears	
	Watercress	Persimmons	
		Pineapples	
		Plantains	
		Plums	
		Quinces	
		Raspberries	
		Star fruit	
		Strawberries	
		Tomatoes	

Table taken from Produce Marketing Association *Fresh Produce Manual* November 2022.

Turn Down the Dial (On Your Fridge)

According to 'Love Food, Hate Waste' the average UK fridge is 2°C too warm. By making sure your fridge is below 5°C, you can help some foods last up to three days longer (use a thermometer for accuracy, see page 60).

You'll find that the temperature varies depending on where you put the sensor(s) in your fridge, so it'll be warmest in the door and towards the top, whilst coldest on the bottom shelf and in the crisper drawer(s). The back of your fridge will also be colder than the front of the shelves.

Location, Location, Location

Where you store different foods in your fridge really matters. Check out the diagram opposite to see what should be stored where, both to keep your food at its freshest and to reduce the risk of cross-contamination.

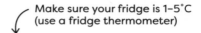

Make sure your fridge is 1–5°C
(use a fridge thermometer)

1. Top shelf
Cooked & ready-
to-eat foods

2. Middle shelf
Dairy products
& eggs (or dairy
substitutes)

3. Bottom shelf
Raw meat & fish
(wrapped)

4. Drawers
Fruit & vegetables

5. Door
Condiments, jams,
juices & sauces

WHY YOU SHOULD KEEP EGGS IN THE FRIDGE

I know this one could kick off quite the debate as people are often passionate about where they store their eggs! The advice on this varies across the world because of different production methods, but here in the UK the official advice (from British Lion eggs) is to keep your eggs in the fridge in their original packaging.

This is because eggshells have tiny pores which bacteria and smells can seep through, especially if the eggs fluctuate in temperature. Keeping them in their original carton will help to stop smells from transferring, and storing them at a consistent temperature under 20°C reduces any safety risks and helps them stay fresh for longer. If you have a cool pantry to store them in, this could also be an option, but the temperature of a normal kitchen will usually fluctuate too much.

And if you're wondering why they're kept on the shelf and not in a fridge in supermarkets, it's because they're air-conditioned!

Don't Bin Your Best Befores

If you don't already know the difference between sell-by, use-by and best before dates, listen up!

First of all, any sell-by dates on products can be completely ignored, as this information is only there for the retailer. It *is* important though to understand the difference between best before and use-by dates.

Best before dates are simply there to indicate the quality of the product. As the name suggests, these foods are best eaten before the date printed on the packet. But as long as there isn't any sign of mould or decay, these foods will be perfectly safe to eat after this date. The kinds of products you might find best before dates on are fruit and veg, bread and chocolate. If you're guilty of throwing food away because it's reached its best before date, you can immediately start to save yourself some cash by using your senses to assess whether it's still okay to eat.

Use-by dates, however, *are* there for our safety and should be stuck to even if the food in the packet appears okay. This is because use-by dates are applied to higher-risk products that have a tendency to carry pathogenic bacteria (see page 111).

As long as you store these foods following the instructions on the packet (i.e. refrigerating at below

5°C), they should remain safe up until and including the use-by date. You can even freeze these foods on this date as long as there are no signs of decay.

If you know you won't use something before the use-by date, I recommend freezing it as soon as possible to ensure it's the best quality it can be and to minimise the risk of any harmful bacteria developing (for example, if your fridge was not cold enough).

A Final Word

I'm hoping that if you've made it this far, you've already started implementing some changes in your planning, shopping, prepping and cooking, and that your confidence around using your freezer is growing every day! However you choose to make your freezer work for you, you should now feel better equipped to use the space effectively and more confident in making use of the foods in your Freezer Stash.

There'll no doubt be days when food still gets wasted, or your freezer is chaos, but you've got the tools now to regain control quickly. If you start to feel that what you're doing isn't working for you anymore, be sure to revisit this book to find a new way forward so you can keep on benefiting from that magical pause button in your kitchen.

And please do share your wins and tag me on Instagram @thefullfreezer – I love to see The Full Freezer Method in action!

Happy freezing!

Kate xx

THE FREEZER GEEK'S QUICK REFERENCE GUIDE: *What the Heck Can You Freeze Anyway?*

Okay, okay, I guess what you really want to know is . . .

'Can I actually freeze [insert name of random food here]?!'

Let me remind you, almost everything can be frozen, so the answer is most likely 'yes!'. There are some foods, however, that don't react well to freezing and so cannot be 'saved' (I'm looking at you, mayonnaise!).

While some foods are purposefully stocked in our freezers, there'll be others that are an experiment (because the food would have otherwise ended up in the bin). Don't forget the 'Five Golden Rules' from page 54 when following the advice given over the coming pages.

In this section, I've done my best to cover as many foods as possible (there are over 700 in here for you!), but I've stuck to the quickest and easiest freezing options for each one. There may be other ways you could freeze your food, which might help preserve them for longer (such as freezing fruit in sugar or syrup), but I want to minimise the hurdles that might get in your way and encourage you to use what you freeze regularly.

For the same reason, I haven't included guidance on how long foods can be frozen for – as long as you follow the food safety advice in this book, your food should be safe in the freezer almost indefinitely (but as you know by now, the quality will deteriorate). The best rule of thumb is to use everything within 3–6 months (unless I've flagged the food as needing to be used up sooner). Please don't immediately throw anything away after this time unless there are clear signs it's spoiled, or you have reason to believe it's unsafe.

The whole premise of The Full Freezer Method is to use your freezer as a pause button, not for long-term storage! Why buy something if you're not planning to eat it within the next few months (unless you live somewhere incredibly remote and have *lots* of freezer space).

It's important to make sure you follow any freezing

advice from the manufacturer or producer too, as products may have been previously frozen. I have flagged this up several times throughout the following sections to remind you not just to ask, but to check if their advice is for safety or quality purposes. Often products will be labelled 'do not freeze' as the container is unsuitable, or the product will be lower quality after freezing, but that doesn't mean you can't try.

I've included a few extra notes in each section, to provide you with some useful information, but please don't treat this reference guide as the be-all and end-all. It's certainly good advice to follow (even if I do say so myself), but if you want to try a different approach and it works for you, that's great.

Each section then includes lists of the relevant foods with symbols to give you an at-a-glance overview of your options. These vary from section to section, but I've included a key on pages 200–1 so you can use that to decipher what I'm on about. Please note that when it comes to the ticks, you don't need to do everything. For example, berries can be open-frozen or made into a purée and frozen flat or in cubes. And meats *can* be marinated before freezing, but they don't *have* to be.

And please be aware that I've not included a symbol for putting the food into a freezer bag once you've open-frozen or cube-frozen as, quite frankly, that is a given.

If the food is something that won't freeze solid, or can't be open- or flat-frozen, you'll see that I've indicated to freeze it in small pots or appropriately sized tubs, which can then be stored in a freezer bag for an extra layer of protection. Be sure to read the introduction to each section for important info on what is outlined.

If you're a stickler for correctly categorising foods, please be aware that these sections are intentionally organised by foods that are frozen in a similar way. For example, olives are technically classified as a 'stone fruit' even though we don't keep them in our fruit bowls. Tomatoes and rhubarb are fruit, but they're in there with the veggies! When looking for something specific, I strongly recommend you jump to the Index on page 304 to locate whatever you're after.

KEY

SYMBOL	MEANING
	Wash and dry
	Remove stone/core/seeds
	Drain any water/juices (if edible, they can be flat-frozen or cube-frozen)
	Peel/Remove rind
	Trim and cut into bize-size pieces/slices/wedges/cut in half (usable portions)

	Separate before freezing (layer with sheets of baking parchment to keep separate)
	Whisk
	Grate or crumble
	Preserve colour with lemon juice
	Add salt or sugar
	Marinate
	Wrap in heavy-duty foil or cling film (optional but reduces the risk of freezer burn, see page 56)
	Vacuum-seal (see pages 84–5)
	Cool before freezing (if home-baked/home-cooked, see page 102)
	Blanch (see page 78)
O.F.	Open-freeze (see page 70)
F.F.	Flat-freeze (see page 72)
	Cube-freeze (see page 75)
	Freeze in small pots
	Freeze in containers
	Freeze ready-to-eat (for example, ice lollies)

Also, right at the end of this guide is a list of foods that don't freeze well (see the 'What Can't You Freeze' section on pages 298–300). That's not necessarily because they're unsafe to freeze, but because they won't freeze well and will be difficult to use in an appetising way after freezing. If you want to give it a go, then by all means try it, but don't say I didn't warn you!

Animal Products & Alternatives

Plant-based Protein

If you're vegan or vegetarian, I'll save you from having to skim through this section and tell you what you need to know right up front.

There are ever-increasing numbers of products on the market, so the best advice I can give is to always check directly with the manufacturer about whether their products are suitable for freezing. There are often contact details on the packaging, but if not, their website should have a contact form. Some manufacturers give clear guidance on the packaging, but if not, ask if you *can* freeze their product – if the answer is 'no', then ask whether this is due to *safety* or *quality* reasons. It's also worth finding out whether a fresh product can be cooked and frozen again in a meal (for example, if you want to use frozen veggie mince in a Bolognese).

As production processes may change, I can't list specific products and brands here, but I have included four common meat alternatives and you'll find beans, pulses and veggies further on in the section.

It's a good idea to portion out any 'blocks', with how you want to use them in mind (sliced, cubed, torn or crumbled). You can also marinade before or after freezing, although it's recommended that you freeze, thaw, press and then marinate for greater absorption of the marinade. Leftovers should also be safe to freeze as long as you've followed food safety rules (see page 101).

PLANT-BASED PROTEINS

			O.F.	F.F.	
Seitan	✓	✓	✓	-	✓
Soya mince, cooked	-	✓	-	✓	-
Tempeh	✓	✓	✓	-	✓
Tofu	✓	✓	✓	-	✓

Raw Meat, Game & Poultry

I've previously mentioned that meat can be frozen in joints, individual portions (like steaks or chops), small pieces or as mince. The decision you need to make is whether you want to freeze your meat in a way that maximises its quality and allows you to store it for longer, or in a way that makes it easy to defrost and cook.

From a quality perspective, the best way to preserve

meat in the freezer is to remove any excess fat (as this can become rancid if frozen for too long), freeze it in as large a piece as possible and vacuum-seal it (alternatively, buy a vacuum-packed joint that is labelled as suitable for freezing). However, most of us don't have the space for large, vac-packed joints in our freezer, nor do we often find ourselves cooking one big joint of meat (except maybe for a Sunday dinner, but then it's more likely to be bought fresh).

So, if you find yourself buying portions of meat and then only need to feed a few people, I strongly advise that you prioritise portioning it up before freezing. For example, a chicken breast that has been butterflied and flat-frozen (see illustration below), or diced and open-frozen, is much quicker to defrost than a pack of four chicken breasts frozen in a solid block.

Similarly, splitting up your large pack of minced meats into smaller flat-frozen portions will speed up defrosting, and allow you to fit more in your freezer.

The principle of portioning up and individually freezing meat applies to any meats that you want to use in small quantities, including sausages, burgers and chops. You need to be careful of cross-contamination (never freeze raw meat alongside ready-to-eat foods), and in an ideal world you'd have a designated space for freezing raw meats. For most people, this won't be realistic, so the best option is to freeze small pieces on a plastic plate lined with disposable baking parchment. Wrap the baking parchment over the food and then enclose this in a freezer bag.

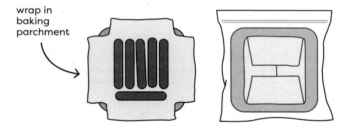

wrap in baking parchment

I must stress that freezing meat in small pieces without vacuum-packing it first makes it more susceptible to freezer burn. One step you can take to minimise this is to coat the pieces of meat in oil or a marinade before open-freezing (or freeze in usable quantities in a sauce).

The simplest option is to use spray oil to coat the pieces (if you're planning to cook in an air fryer or non-stick pan, don't use a low-calorie oil spray as they contain lecithin which damages the non-stick coating). Once they're frozen solid, the pieces of meat can be wrapped in heavy-duty foil before storing in a freezer bag. If you do this, note on the bag what you've coated the meat in as it's easy to forget – you don't want to assume your meat is freezer burnt, when it actually has a protective layer of oil frozen around it.

Although my preference is to freeze meat in small pieces and avoid vacuum-sealing, I've summarised the various cuts of meats so you have a full picture. Note: when freezing whole joints, pop the vacuum-sealed packs (home, or store-bought) inside a large freezer bag if possible for an extra layer of protection.

IMPORTANT: DON'T WASH

I've included the 'wash and dry' symbol intentionally in the table on pages 208–11 to indicate that you should *not* wash any meat before cooking. This is because it leads to bacteria being spread around the kitchen and the cross-contamination of other foods.

LARGE JOINTS & WHOLE BIRDS

	🧺	🥣	🥩
Beef	-	✓	✓
Chicken	-	✓	✓
Duck	-	✓	✓
Guinea fowl	-	✓	✓
Lamb	-	✓	✓
Pork	-	✓	✓
Turkey	-	✓	✓
Veal	-	✓	✓
Venison	-	✓	✓

SMALL CUTS (E.G. STEAKS, CHOPS, CUBES)

	🧺	🔪	🥣	O.F.	F.F.	🧻	🥩
Beef	-	✓	✓	✓	✓	✓	✓
Chicken	-	✓	✓	✓	✓	✓	✓
Lamb	-	✓	✓	✓	✓	✓	✓
Pork	-	✓	✓	✓	✓	✓	✓

SMALL CUTS cont.

	🪣	🔪	🥣	O.F.	F.F.	▭	🍖
Turkey	-	✓	✓	✓	✓	✓	✓
Veal	-	✓	✓	✓	✓	✓	✓
Venison	-	✓	✓	✓	✓	✓	✓

GROUND MEATS & POULTRY*

	🪣	🥣	O.F.	F.F.
Beef	-	✓	✓ (meatballs or burgers)	✓
Chicken	-	✓	✓ (meatballs or burgers)	✓
Lamb	-	✓	✓ (meatballs or burgers)	✓
Pork	-	✓	✓ (meatballs or burgers)	✓
Turkey	-	✓	✓ (meatballs or burgers)	✓
Veal	-	✓	✓ (meatballs or burgers)	✓
Venison	-	✓	✓ (meatballs or burgers)	✓

*IMPORTANT: Ground meat products such as burgers must always be cooked through fully. With anything minced, any bacteria on the surface will be spread throughout the meat so needs to be killed off.

TOP TIP

Some supermarkets now stock 'cook from frozen' meats. These are super convenient, particularly the cook from frozen mince, but they can fill up your freezer very quickly, so make sure you've got plenty of space before you go on a shopping spree!

PROCESSED MEATS & MORE*

	🛁	🥣	🔪	O.F.	F.F.	⬜	▭
Bacon (smoked), sliced or diced (2 months)	-	-	-	✓	✓	-	✓
Bacon (unsmoked), sliced or diced (1 month)	-	-	-	✓	✓	-	✓
Black pudding (2 months)	-	-	✓	✓	-	-	✓
Bone broth	-	-	-	-	✓	✓	-
Bratwurst	-	-	✓	✓	-	-	✓

PROCESSED MEATS cont.

	⊔	🥣	🔪	O.F.	F.F.	⬡	▭
Chorizo	-	-	✓	✓	-	-	✓
Dripping	-	-	✓	✓	-	✓	-
Duck fat	-	-	-	-	✓	✓	-
Goose fat	-	-	-	-	✓	✓	-
Haggis	-	-	-	-	-	-	✓
Hot-dog sausages (2 months)	-	-	-	✓	-	-	✓
Kidneys	-	✓	✓	✓	-	-	✓
Lard (shortening)	-	-	✓	✓	-	✓	-
Liver (raw)	-	✓	✓	✓	-	-	-
'Nduja (1 month)	-	-	✓	✓	-	-	✓
Pancetta	-	-	✓	✓	-	-	✓
Pepperoni (2 months)	-	-	-	✓	-	-	✓
Pigs-in-blankets (1 month)	-	-	-	✓	-	-	✓
Sausagemeat (2 months)	-	-	✓	✓	✓	-	✓
Sausages (2 months)	-	✓	-	✓	-	-	✓

*Because these foods are usually used in small quantities, vacuum-sealing isn't realistic in most cases. If desired, you can wrap items in foil once they're frozen to help protect them, then enclose in a freezer bag.

Raw Fish & Shellfish

When it comes to creatures of the sea, it might surprise you to find out that many of the 'fresh' fish in our supermarket have actually been previously frozen. If they've been imported, this is to preserve them, but in other cases, it's a necessary requirement to kill off possible parasites (particularly if the fish will be eaten cold, such as in sushi or sashimi).

The fact that they've been previously frozen doesn't mean that we can't freeze these products, as they're frozen and defrosted under very controlled conditions, but it's important to always check the packaging or speak to your fishmonger to make sure.

As with meat, I recommend freezing fish in usable portions (taking the same safety precautions to avoid cross-contamination). Cut up any whole fish or large cuts into amounts that you're actually likely to use in one go.

Vacuum-sealing helps to prolong the life of your fish in the freezer (particularly fatty fish like mackerel), but I simply open-freeze individual fillets or pieces and then store them in a freezer bag, wrapping them in foil if they'll be frozen for more than a week or two.

You can also freeze your fish in a marinade, if you like, but keep in mind that this will take up more space.

To minimise the bulk, I place the marinade and fillets in a freezer bag, coat the fillets fully and then lay the bag out on a tray, separating the fillets from each other so the whole lot won't need defrosting when you want one.

Another option is to 'ice glaze' your fish, whereby you dip it in cold water then open-freeze, dip it again and open-freeze again, then repeat this until there's a protective coating of ice (around 5mm) surrounding the fish to help lock in the moisture.

RAW FISH

	🧺	🔪	🥣	O.F.	📄	🥩
Bass	-	✓	✓	✓	✓	✓
Bream (2 months)	-	✓	✓	✓	✓	✓
Cod	-	✓	✓	✓	✓	✓
Haddock	-	✓	✓	✓	✓	✓
Hake	-	✓	✓	✓	✓	✓
Kippers	-	✓	✓	✓	✓	✓
Mackerel (2 months)	-	✓	✓	✓	✓	✓
Plaice	-	✓	✓	✓	✓	✓
Salmon (2 months)	-	✓	✓	✓	✓	✓

RAW FISH cont.

	⊔	🔪	🥣	O.F.	▭	🥩
Sole	–	✓	✓	✓	✓	✓
Swordfish	–	✓	✓	✓	✓	✓
Trout (2 months)	–	–	✓	✓	✓	✓
Tuna (2 months)	–	✓	✓	✓	✓	✓

RAW SHELLFISH

	⊔	🔪	🥣	O.F.	▭	🥩
Prawns, unpeeled (1 month)	✓	–	–	✓	✓	✓
Prawns, peeled (1 month)	–	–	✓	✓	✓	✓
Scallops (1 month)	–	–	✓	✓	✓	✓
Scampi, breaded (1 month)	–	–	–	✓	✓	✓

A QUICK WORD ON SHELLFISH

It is possible to freeze other shellfish such as crab, lobster, mussels and oysters (as well as those listed on page 214), but you're always going to be better off eating them fresh or buying ready-frozen products to minimise risk. Shellfish can cause severe food poisoning if not handled correctly, so my advice in these cases is to leave it to the experts.

If you do choose to freeze any of the above items, it's best to do so on the day of purchase. It's also a good idea to always store fish and shellfish towards the back of your freezer to keep it as cold as possible as the temperature will fluctuate at the front of the drawers when the door is opened.

Cooked Meat, Poultry, Fish & Shellfish

The most important thing to remember when freezing cooked meat, poultry or fish is that you won't be able to reheat any dish that these are used in. This is because you will have already reheated them when cooking the dish. If you're using pre-cooked ingredients, you need to aim to have no leftovers!

The most practical approach is to cut foods into small pieces so you can use only as much as you need (for example, adding a few pieces of frozen ham to an omelette or some cooked chicken to a risotto). This also means cooked meats and fish are very prone to freezer burn and shouldn't be stored for very long. You can wrap them in foil within the freezer bag for an extra layer of protection or vacuum-seal them in usable portions if you know how much you're likely to use (again, I avoid this to save on single-use plastic).

If you're freezing slices of meats such as beef, chicken or turkey, flat-freezing them in a sauce or gravy is a great way to reduce the risk of freezer burn and keep them moist (it does mean you have to thaw them in the fridge overnight though, and of course you can't alter the portion size to suit your appetite).

Having a selection of cooked meats and fish in your freezer is particularly handy if you're catering mainly for vegetarian or vegan diets but also the occasional meat-eaters. You can simply cook a veggie/vegan dish, then add the cooked meat or fish after dishing it up for everyone else. Either defrost the meat or fish in advance in the fridge and eat cold, or heat through thoroughly, which can be done from frozen if the pieces are small – don't forget to use your food probe thermometer! If you are making something like an omelette which could become overcooked whilst trying to get your meat to a safe temperature, it's a good idea to heat up your meat first, then add your other ingredients. And remember, if you are freezing shop-bought cooked meats or fish, reach out to the producer to check it's safe to freeze.

COOKED MEATS & POULTRY

	🌡*	🔪	O.F.	▯	🍖
Bacon bits or slices, cooked (2 months)	✓	✓	✓	✓	✓
Beef, cooked (1 month)	✓	✓	✓	✓	✓
Chicken, cooked (1 month)	✓	✓	✓	✓	✓
Duck, cooked	✓	✓	✓	✓	✓
Ham, cooked (1 month)	✓	✓	✓	✓	✓
Guinea fowl, cooked	✓	✓	✓	✓	✓

COOKED MEATS & POULTRY cont.

	🌡*	🔪	O.F.	▭	◎
Lamb, cooked (1 month)	✓	✓	✓	✓	✓
Liver (2 months)	✓	✓	✓	✓	✓
Pâté (2 months)	✓	✓	✓	✓	✓
Pastrami (2 months)	✓	✓	✓	✓	✓
Pork, cooked (1 month)	✓	✓	✓	✓	✓
Prosciutto (1 month)	-	✓	✓	✓	✓
Salt beef (1 month)	✓	✓	✓	✓	✓
Sausages, cooked (1 month)	✓	✓	✓	✓	✓
Turkey, cooked (1 month)	✓	✓	✓	✓	✓
Veal, cooked (2 months)	✓	✓	✓	✓	✓
Venison, cooked (2 months)	✓	✓	✓	✓	✓

For Tinned Meats see the 'Pantry' section on page 293

COOKED & READY-TO-EAT FISH & SHELLFISH

	🌡 *	🔪	O.F.	▭	◉
Bass, cooked (2 months)	✓	✓	✓	✓	✓
Bream, cooked (2 months)	✓	✓	✓	✓	✓
Cod, cooked (2 months)	✓	✓	✓	✓	✓
Haddock, cooked (2 months)	✓	✓	✓	✓	✓
Hake, cooked (2 months)	✓	✓	✓	✓	✓
Mackerel, hot smoked (1 month)	✓	✓	✓	✓	✓
Plaice, cooked (2 months)	✓	✓	✓	✓	✓
Prawns, cooked (2–3 months)	✓	-	✓	✓	✓
Salmon, cooked (2 months)	✓	✓	✓	✓	✓
Salmon, cold smoked*	✓	✓	-	✓	✓
Salmon, hot smoked (2 months)	✓	✓	✓	✓	✓
Sole, cooked (2 months)	✓	✓	✓	✓	✓
Swordfish, cooked (2 months)	✓	✓	✓	✓	✓
Trout, cooked (2 months)	✓	✓	✓	✓	✓
Tuna, cooked (2 months)	✓	✓	✓	✓	✓

For Tinned Fish see the 'Pantry' section on page 293

*If you know you'll use all of your cold smoked salmon in one go, you're best freezing it in its original packaging to better preserve the quality! Always check the packaging to make sure it's safe for freezing in case it's been frozen previously.

Eggs

If you ever end up with more eggs than you need then freezing them is a fab option, just don't freeze them in their shells as they'll crack and this can lead to bacteria on the outside of the egg transferring to the inside.

My preference is to whisk up whole eggs and freeze them flat so they take up little space and can be defrosted quickly (I usually freeze them in portions of two or three eggs). If you prefer, you can freeze individual eggs in silicone muffin cases or baby weaning trays, but I do encourage you to whisk them before freezing as they become difficult to combine after. Also, always make a note of the quantity you've frozen in case you decide to use them for baking (it might be useful to know that an average egg measures about 3 tablespoons or 45ml).

If you have only yolks or whites leftover from baking these can also be frozen. The whites will be fine as they are, but it's a good idea to add a pinch of salt or half a teaspoon of sugar per yolk, depending on whether you're planning to use them in a sweet or savoury dish. This helps to stop the yolk from becoming too gloopy and hard to use.

When it comes to cooked eggs, boiled eggs don't freeze well (more on this on page 298), but you can absolutely freeze scrambled eggs, omelettes, frittatas and other egg-based delights. Depending on how you're planning on using these, you may wish to flat-freeze or slice into portions before open-freezing and transferring to a freezer bag (wrapping in foil if you want to store for a while).

EGGS

				O.F.	F.F.		
Whole eggs (uncooked)	-	✓	-	-	✓	✓	-
Egg yolk (uncooked)	-	✓	✓	-	✓	✓	-
Egg white (uncooked)	-	-	-	-	✓	✓	-
Whole eggs (cooked)	✓	-	-	✓	✓	-	✓

Baked Goods

Most people are aware that baked goods can be frozen, but I often read comments from people about not having space, or their unsuccessful freezing attempts.

You can generally freeze homemade or shop-bought baked goods. If they're homemade, be sure to cool your bakes fully before putting them in the freezer, and if they're shop-bought, check the packaging for a 'not suitable for freezing' label. If you find one of these, reach out to the manufacturer to check if this is for quality or safety reasons.

This section mostly focuses on freezing items that have already been baked (whether at home or by a bakery), but it's also possible to freeze dough and batters. Always freeze in usable portions and thaw fully before baking. And don't forget 'To Test For Success' (see page 55), as it's always a good idea to do a small test run before baking any large batches!

If you're limited in freezer space, consider turning whatever you've got into breadcrumbs (see page 224) so it can be flat-frozen in a freezer bag. This can of course be done with sliced bread, but don't forget you can do the same with pastries like croissants, buns and rolls as toppings for any savoury or sweet pies or bakes.

You could even blitz up cake to make cake pops later, or serve sprinkled over ice cream.

When it comes to storing your baked goods, if they'll only be frozen for a month or two then you can get away with popping them in a freezer bag (just be sure to open-freeze anything that might stick together such as slices of cake). If you'll be storing items for longer, then it's a good idea to wrap bakes individually in baking parchment and heavy-duty foil to protect them from freezer burn.

Frozen baked goods are one of the rare foods that can be thawed at room temperature, but you do have to be careful of them drying out. Keep them sealed in a freezer bag while thawing and place a sheet of kitchen paper under them inside the bag to absorb any moisture. Alternatively, baked goods can be removed from the freezer bag and microwaved on the defrost setting in 10-second bursts or placed in a warm oven for 5–10 minutes (wrap in foil to avoid them going crunchy). Alternatively, toast them straight from frozen.

Breads, Buns & More

If you don't have much freezer space and you're not keen on breadcrumbs, consider separating whatever you've got into smaller quantities to freeze. For example, if you always waste the last few slices of a loaf of bread, remove four or eight slices when you open your loaf and freeze them flat in a large freezer bag or several small ones. You don't need to freeze the whole loaf as it is!

To save time when thawing, rolls, bagels and buns should also be cut in half *before* freezing. The same goes for cutting any unsliced bread or baguettes into slices. This way they can be defrosted much faster and even toasted straight from frozen. Croissants are an exception to this one though – they are *far* easier to cut in half when frozen!

It's perfectly safe to store baked goods in your freezer for quite a while, but it's worth noting that any crusty or flaky items will start to lose their outer layer quite quickly. Of course, this doesn't mean you have to bin them, but they may be best used in a dish where their quality isn't as important.

BREADS

	🌡*	🔪	O.F.	▭
Bagel	✓	✓	✓	✓
Baguette (1 week)	✓	✓	✓	✓
Blinis	✓	-	✓	✓
Breadcrumbs (fresh)	-	-	-	✓
Brioche	✓	✓	✓	✓

BREADS cont.

	![thermometer]*	![knife]	O.F.	![freezer bag]
Challah	✓	✓	✓	✓
Ciabatta	✓	✓	✓	✓
Croutons (1–2 months)	✓	-	✓	✓
Focaccia (1 month)	✓	✓	✓	✓
Panettone	✓	✓	✓	✓
Panini (2 months)	✓	✓	✓	✓
Part-baked bread (1 month)	-	✓	✓	✓
Pita bread	✓	-	✓	✓
Pretzels	✓	✓	✓	✓
Rye bread	✓	✓	✓	✓
Scones	✓	✓	✓	✓
Sliced bread	✓	-	✓	✓
Soda bread	✓	✓	✓	✓
Soft bread & rolls	✓	✓	✓	✓
Sourdough	✓	✓	✓	✓
Yorkshire puddings (2–3 months)	✓	-	✓	✓

BUNS & SWEET BREADS

	🌡️*	🔪	O.F.	▭
Buns, bao	✓	–	✓	✓
Buns, Belgian	✓	✓	✓	✓
Buns, burger	✓	✓	✓	✓
Buns, Chelsea	✓	✓	✓	✓
Buns, currant	✓	✓	✓	✓
Buns, hot cross	✓	✓	✓	✓
Cake, rock	✓	✓	✓	✓
Cake, Welsh	✓	✓	✓	✓
Rolls, cinnamon (2 months)	✓	✓	✓	✓
Teacakes	✓	✓	✓	✓

PASTRIES

	🌡️*	🔪	O.F.	▭
Baklava	✓	–	✓	✓
Churros (1 month)	✓	✓	✓	✓
Croissants	✓	–	✓	✓

PASTRIES cont.

	🌡*	🔪	O.F.	📜
Danish pastries	✓	✓	✓	✓
Doughnuts (incl. jam)	✓	-	✓	✓
Éclairs (2 months)	✓	-	✓	✓
Pain au chocolat	✓	-	✓	✓
Pain au raisins (2 months)	✓	-	✓	✓
Profiteroles	✓	-	✓	✓
Turnovers (1 month)	✓	-	✓	✓
Yum Yums	✓	-	✓	✓

PASTRY (UNBAKED)

	🔪	O.F.	F.F.	📜
Choux pastry	✓	✓	✓	✓
Filo pastry	✓	✓	✓	✓
Flaky pastry (aka rough-puff)	✓	✓	✓	✓
Puff pastry	✓	✓	✓	✓
Shortcrust pastry	✓	✓	✓	✓

Pancakes & Flatbreads

For items like pancakes and wraps, always put them on a flat surface to freeze them (it could be a freezing tray (see page 71), baking tray, chopping board, picnic plate or even just the freezer shelf or drawer). This helps to ensure they take up as little space as possible and they're less likely to end up breaking.

Always separate slices, pancakes and wraps before freezing (you may want to put baking parchment between each one to ensure they don't stick). If they go in the freezer stuck together, it's unlikely that you'll be able to successfully prise them apart without breaking them and then you'll have to defrost them all whether you need to or not. Also, don't put anything on top of them while freezing as this may cause them to stick back together!

PANCAKES & FLATBREADS

	🌡*	🔪	🍳	O.F.	F.F.	📄
American pancakes	✓	-	✓	✓	-	✓
Banana pancakes	✓	-	✓	✓	-	✓
Chapati	✓	-	✓	✓	-	✓

PANCAKES & FLATBREADS cont.

	🌡*	🔪	🍶	O.F.	F.F.	📄
Crêpes	✓	-	✓	✓	-	✓
Crumpets	✓	-	✓	✓	-	✓
English muffins	✓	✓	✓	✓	-	✓
Flatbread	✓	-	✓	✓	-	✓
Naan bread	✓	-	✓	✓	-	✓
Pancake batter	-	-	-	-	✓	-
Pancakes (filled) (2 months)	-	-	-	✓	-	✓
Pancakes (unfilled)	✓	-	✓	✓	-	✓
Tortillas (corn or flour)	✓	-	✓	✓	-	✓
Waffles (2 months)	✓	-	✓	✓	-	✓

Cakes & More

Much the same as with bread, it's a good idea to cut any leftover cake up into portions too. Far better to be able to just grab a slice at a time than have to defrost the whole lot in one go!

Some cakes are surprisingly tasty straight from the freezer, just be sure to check how solidly your snack has frozen before biting into it – I take no responsibility for any broken teeth! Remember, if the cake has been gifted to you or bought from a shop, check if it has previously been frozen.

CAKES & MORE*

	🌡*	🔪	O.F.	F.F.	▭
Angel cake	✓	✓	✓	-	✓
Banana bread	✓	✓	✓	-	✓
Brownies	✓	✓	✓	-	✓
Cake mixture/batter (uncooked) (2 months)	-	-	-	✓	-
Cake pops	✓	-	✓	-	✓
Carrot cake	✓	✓	✓	-	✓
Chocolate cake	✓	✓	✓	-	✓
Christmas cake	✓	✓	✓	-	✓
Coffee cake	✓	✓	✓	-	✓
Courgette cake (1 month)	✓	✓	✓	-	✓
Dundee cake	✓	✓	✓	-	✓
Eccles cake	✓	✓	✓	-	✓
Flapjacks	✓	✓	✓	-	✓

CAKES & MORE cont.

	🌡*	🔪	O.F.	F.F.	🗒
Fruit cake (light)	✓	✓	✓	-	✓
Lemon cake	✓	✓	✓	-	✓
Madeira cake	✓	✓	✓	-	✓
Muffins (2 months)	✓	-	✓	-	✓
Polenta cake	✓	✓	✓	-	✓
Pound cake	✓	✓	✓	-	✓
Red velvet cake	✓	✓	✓	-	✓
Rocky road	✓	✓	✓	-	✓
Roulade (1 month)	✓	✓	✓	-	✓
Rum babas	✓	-	✓	-	✓
Stollen	✓	✓	✓	-	✓
Vanilla cake	✓	✓	✓	-	✓

*If you want to prep and freeze a cake in advance for a special occasion you can absolutely do this, I would be cautious of freezing your cakes fully iced and decorated though. Whilst icing can be frozen, it will soften on thawing so you may lose definition on your cake. Any colouring used is at risk of running too. If you have picked up a (suitable for freezing) discounted party cake in the supermarket then it may be worth the risk, but for anything hand decorated I would only freeze the cake sponge in advance, then thaw and decorate.

BISCUITS & COOKIES

	🌡*	🔪	O.F.	▯
Amaretti	✓	-	-	✓
Biscotti	✓	-	-	✓
Biscuits	✓	-	-	✓
Chocolate Chip Cookies	✓	-	-	✓
Cookie Dough	-	✓	✓	✓
Gingerbread	✓	-	-	✓
Iced Cookies	✓	-	✓	✓
Macarons	✓	-	✓	✓
Millionaire's Shortbread	✓	✓	✓	✓
Oatcakes (Scottish)	✓	-	-	✓
Shortbread	✓	✓	-	✓
Stroopwafels	✓	-	-	✓
Tiffin	✓	-	✓	✓
Viennese Whirls	✓	✓	-	✓

Dairy & Dairy Substitutes

Milks, Creams & More

If you have surplus dairy or dairy substitutes, the good news is that, generally speaking, you can safely freeze them. The bad news is that a lot of items will not react overly well to freezing – milks, creams and yoghurts are likely to separate and cheeses may become crumbly and less creamy.

It does *not*, however, mean you shouldn't freeze them! Remember, if the alternative is to pour your milk away, you might as well give it a go. I will add the caveat that if you're freezing a dairy substitute, it's always best to check directly with the manufacturer and ask the quality or safety question (see page 199).

The reason that dairy products tend to split is simply because the fats or solids separate from the liquid. In the case of cow's milk, it may become lumpy and even look yellow in colour, which leads a lot of people to think it's spoiled. But after a good shake or a whizz with a hand blender, it'll be back to its usual smooth self (once the froth has died down). If you freeze a dairy product or dairy alternative and it goes lumpy, have a go at recombining it (or in the case of nut milks, re-strain it through a cheesecloth) before you give up on it, then use it as if it were fresh (ideally in cooking or smoothies).

The key thing to know about freezing dairy products is that you can't refreeze them and most should be used within 24 hours of defrosting, so stick to freezing portion sizes you can actually consume in that time.

I like to flat-freeze milk in a freezer bag so I can defrost it quickly in a dish of cold water. You can also freeze in cubes, which can be useful for smoothies. I've seen some people suggest that these cubes can be added to your tea or coffee too, so you may like to try this, but I've had varying success, often finding the separated milk curdles in a hot drink.

When it comes to freezing dairy products, it's very much a case of giving it a go and figuring out what works best for you!

MILKS

	F.F.	⬡
Almond milk	✓	✓
Cashew milk	✓	✓
Chocolate milk	✓	✓
Cow's milk	✓	✓
Goat's milk (2 months)	✓	✓

MILKS cont.

	F.F.	❒
Oat milk	✓	✓
Soya milk	✓	✓
UHT milk	✓	✓

CREAMS & MORE

	🥄	F.F.	❒
Buttermilk	-	✓	✓
Clotted cream	-	✓	✓
Crème fraîche	-	✓	✓
Double cream*	✓	✓	✓
Single cream	-	✓	✓
Sour cream	-	✓	✓
Soya cream (1 month)	-	✓	✓
Whipping cream*	✓	✓	✓

*Creams that are made to be whipped are best done so before freezing to avoid them splitting.

Yoghurts

Yoghurts tend to suffer the same splitting issue as other dairy products, although, freezing them so they can be consumed still frozen works surprisingly well! Take a look online for 'yoghurt bark' recipes, or whip up some lollies by mixing together yoghurt, berries and honey and then freezing them in moulds. Frozen cubes can also be added to smoothies, or you can flat-freeze larger quantities of plain yoghurt to use in cooking.

YOGHURT

	F.F.	⬡	🍦
Coconut yoghurt (1 month)	✓	✓	✓
Fromage frais yoghurt	✓	✓	✓
Fruit-flavoured yoghurt (2 months)	✓	✓	✓
Greek yoghurt (2 months)	✓	✓	✓
Natural yoghurt (2 months)	✓	✓	✓

Butters & Spreads

Unlike other dairy products, butters and spreads freeze pretty well! They're usually stable enough to last for a little while (up to three weeks in some cases) in the fridge after thawing, in comparison to most foods that should be eaten within 24 hours. However, always check directly with the manufacturer.

I still prefer to portion out my butter or spreads into usable quantities, such as in small cubes instead of a block.

BUTTERS & SPREADS

	🔪	O.F.	🧊	📦
Flavoured butter (e.g. chilli, garlic, herb, lemon)	✓	✓	✓	✓
Ghee	-	-	✓	-
Low-fat spreads	✓	✓	✓	✓
Margarine	✓	✓	✓	✓
Salted butter	✓	✓	✓	✓
Spreadable butter	✓	✓	✓	✓
Unsalted butter	✓	✓	✓	✓

Cheese

When it comes to cheese, hard cheeses freeze much better than soft. They are best grated (unless you've sliced and frozen it in a sandwich) and used straight from frozen in cooked dishes. You can freeze hard cheese in a block in small usable quantities, if you prefer, although you might find the texture is a bit crumblier than normal. And of course, larger blocks will take quite a while to defrost! If you do freeze it in blocks, always wrap the cheese well and store it inside a freezer bag.

Soft cheeses can be frozen, thawed and eaten as they are, but it's likely the texture and flavour will be altered, so you may prefer to use it in cooking after freezing. They do need to be well wrapped and stored in a freezer bag after open-freezing as they're susceptible to freezer burn.

HARD & SEMI-HARD CHEESES

	🔪	🧀	O.F.	📄
Cheddar	✓	✓	✓	✓
Cheshire	✓	✓	✓	✓
Comté	✓	✓	✓	✓

HARD & SEMI-HARD CHEESES cont.

	🔪	🧀	O.F.	▭
Double Gloucester	✓	✓	✓	✓
Edam	✓	✓	✓	✓
Emmental	✓	✓	✓	✓
Gouda	✓	✓	✓	✓
Grana Padano	✓	✓	✓	✓
Gruyère	✓	✓	✓	✓
Halloumi	✓	✓	✓	✓
Havarti (2 months)	✓	✓	✓	✓
Jarlsberg	✓	✓	✓	✓
Lancashire	✓	✓	✓	✓
Leerdammer	✓	✓	✓	✓
Manchego	✓	✓	✓	✓
Monterey Jack	✓	✓	✓	✓
Parmesan	✓	✓	✓	✓
Pecorino	✓	✓	✓	✓
Raclette	✓	✓	✓	✓

HARD & SEMI-HARD CHEESES cont.

	🔪	🧀	O.F.	▭
Red Leicester	✓	✓	✓	✓
Roquefort	✓	✓	✓	✓
Vegan hard cheese (check with producer)	✓	✓	✓	✓
Wensleydale	✓	✓	✓	✓

SOFT & SEMI-SOFT CHEESES*

	🔪	O.F.	F.F.	◻	▭
Boursin	✓	✓	✓	✓	✓
Brie	✓	✓	-	-	✓
Cambozola	✓	✓	-	-	✓
Camembert	✓	✓	-	-	✓
Cheese spread (2 months)	-	-	✓	✓	✓
Cottage cheese	-	-	✓	✓	✓
Cream cheese	-	-	✓	✓	✓
Feta	✓	✓	-	-	✓
Gorgonzola	✓	✓	-	-	✓

SOFT & SEMI-SOFT CHEESES cont.

	🔪	O.F.	F.F.	🧊	▢
Mascarpone	-	-	✓	✓	✓
Mozzarella	✓	✓	-	-	✓
Paneer	✓	✓	-	-	✓
Reblochon (1 month)	✓	✓	-	-	✓
Ricotta (2 months)	-	-	✓	✓	✓
Stilton	✓	✓	-	-	✓
Taleggio (2 months)	✓	✓	-	-	✓
Vegan soft cheese (check with producer)	-	-	✓	✓	✓

*If you would like to grate a soft cheese for a dish, consider freezing it to firm it up. Just remember, if you want to re-freeze it you'll have to cook it first unless you work very quickly.

Dips, Sauces & More

This is a straightforward section, but there's one important thing to be aware of: Not all dips, spreads and sauces will freeze solid, but this doesn't mean they won't be preserved. It's the cold (-18°C) that stops harmful bacteria from multiplying, not the physical state of the food, so you're still fine to pop these items in the freezer.

What it does mean is that it's always a good idea to test a small amount before filling up your ice-cube tray, because if they don't freeze solid, you won't be able to take them out of the tray. I've indicated on pages 244–6 which foods should be okay to cube-freeze, but this may vary depending on the product you buy or the recipe you follow, so I still recommend testing for yourself. If you are freezing shop-bought products, you should always check directly with the manufacturer if it's safe to do so. For example, freezing store-bought or freshly homemade gravy is usually fine, but gravy made with granules is generally not 'freeze/thaw' stable.

For those foods that don't freeze solid, I recommend using small air-tight tubs (ideally ones that are stackable and clear, so you can see how much is inside) and popping a piece of baking parchment on top of the contents to help protect them from the cold. These tubs should then be stored in a freezer bag to provide an extra layer of protection and keep them stacked together.

When you want to use a sauce, spread or dip, remove the parchment, scoop out what you need, then replace the parchment and return the rest to the freezer. I don't like freezing foods in the glass jars they may have originally come in. Even though this is a great way to avoid using more plastic, not all glass is suitable for the freezer and it can break if it gets knocked about.

It's worth pointing out that those foods that don't freeze solid usually contain a high level of sugar or salt, which are preservatives anyway. Foods containing a lot of vinegar often don't need to be frozen for the same reason. I've listed these anyway as the freezer can give you an extra level of confidence that your food is okay to eat, even if it was opened some time ago.

As with most foods, the consistency and flavour of dips, spreads and sauces can change after freezing and so you may want to use them in dishes (for example, wraps or cooked meals) rather than as dips on their own. Creamy dips are unlikely to freeze particularly well, but if they're otherwise heading to the bin, you could absolutely give it a go! If a creamy sauce has separated, it might be saved by re-blending and heating gently.

For the foods that do freeze as cubes, wrapping them

in a layer of foil and then placing them inside a freezer bag will help prolong their life.

DIPS, SAUCES & MORE

	🌡*	F.F.	⬡	⬠	▭
Almond butter	-	-	✓	-	✓
Apple cider vinegar	-	✓	✓	-	✓
Apple sauce	✓	✓	✓	-	✓
Barbecue sauce	✓	✓	✓	-	✓
Béchamel sauce	✓	✓	✓	-	✓
Bread sauce (1 month)	✓	✓	✓	-	✓
Cashew butter	-	-	✓	-	✓
Cheese sauce	✓	✓	✓	-	✓
Chimichurri	-	✓	✓	-	✓
Chutney	✓	✓	-	✓	-
Cranberry sauce	✓	✓	✓	-	✓
Curry paste	✓	✓	✓	-	✓
Curry sauce	✓	✓	✓	-	✓
Fruit compote	✓	✓	✓	-	✓
Fruit coulis	✓	✓	✓	-	✓

DIPS, SAUCES & MORE cont.

	🌡*	F.F.	⬡	⬭	▭
Gochujang	-	✓	-	✓	✓
Gravy	✓	✓	✓	-	✓
Guacamole	-	✓	✓	-	✓
Harissa paste	-	-	✓	-	✓
Hoisin sauce	✓	-	-	✓	-
Hummus	-	✓	✓	-	✓
Ketchup	✓	✓	✓	-	✓
Kimchi	-	✓	✓	-	✓
Lemon curd	✓	-	-	✓	-
Lemongrass purée	✓	-	✓	-	✓
Maple syrup	-	-	-	✓	-
Marinades	-	✓	✓	✓	✓
Marmite	-	-	✓	✓	✓
Miso paste	✓	-	-	✓	-
Mustard, Dijon	-	-	✓	-	✓
Mustard, English	✓	-	-	✓	✓
Mustard, wholegrain	-	-	✓	-	✓

DIPS, SAUCES & MORE cont.

	🌡*	F.F.	⬡	⬭	▭
Mustard, yellow	✓	-	✓	-	✓
Olive tapenade	-	-	✓	-	✓
Pasta sauce (e.g. Marinara)	✓	✓	✓	-	✓
Peanut butter	-	-	✓	-	✓
Peppercorn sauce	✓	-	✓	-	✓
Pesto, basil	-	✓	✓	-	✓
Pesto, sundried tomato	-	✓	✓	-	✓
Pesto, vegan	-	✓	✓	-	✓
Pizza sauce	✓	✓	✓	-	✓
Salsa verde (2 months)	-	✓	✓	-	✓
Sweet & sour sauce	✓	✓	✓	-	✓
Tahini	-	-	✓	-	✓
Tamarind paste	✓	✓	✓	-	✓
Tomato purée (aka paste)	✓	✓	✓	-	✓
Tomato salsa	-	✓	✓	-	✓

Drinks

The big thing to share here is that if you're freezing any drinks, especially carbonated ones, you *have* to leave space for them to expand. This means no freezing fizzy drinks in cans or sealed bottles as they'll more than likely explode and could damage your freezer.

It's also important to point out that carbonated drinks won't stay fizzy after freezing, so you're really only saving them for the taste and to avoid waste!

You can absolutely freeze and thaw your drinks just for drinking, but some may be far less enjoyable after freezing – wine in particular tends to suffer, so I often use it to cook with straight from frozen. There's no reason you can't try using some white or rosé wine frozen into ice cubes to keep your wine cool on a hot day though; just make sure you try it with a small glass first and remember to label exactly what your frozen wine is!

Fruit juices may also split after freezing – a good stir or shake should rectify this (if necessary, you could use a handheld blender to whizz it back together). Some shop-bought fruit juices may say on the packaging that they should not be frozen, so just drop the manufacturer a line to check if this is for safety or quality reasons – sometimes it's just because the packaging isn't suitable for freezing.

It's worth noting that boozy drinks won't freeze completely solid (if at all), so only freeze them in lidded ice-cube trays that you're happy to keep in the freezer, or flat-freeze in bags in usable quantities.

IMPORTANT: FREEZING DRINKS

Never freeze drinks from a container that you've already drunk from. You'll have introduced bacteria to the drink when sipping, which could multiply when thawing it out later and might make you (or someone else in your home) sick.

FRUIT JUICE

	F.F.	🧊	🍦
Apple juice	✓	✓	✓
Cranberry juice	✓	✓	✓
Grapefruit juice	✓	✓	✓
Guava juice	✓	✓	✓
Lychee juice	✓	✓	✓
Mango juice	✓	✓	✓
Orange juice	✓	✓	✓
Passionfruit juice	✓	✓	✓
Pineapple juice	✓	✓	✓
Pomegranate juice	✓	✓	✓
Prune juice	✓	✓	✓
Tomato juice	✓	✓	✓

FIZZY DRINKS (NOT IN CANS OR SEALED BOTTLES)*

	F.F.	❑	🍭
Cola (1 month)	✓	✓	✓
Dr Pepper (1 month)	✓	✓	✓
Ginger beer (1 month)	✓	✓	✓
Lemonade (1 month)	✓	✓	✓
Lucozade (1 month)	✓	✓	✓
Orange pop (1 month)	✓	✓	✓

*A great option for fizzy drinks other than as lollies is to make granita. This is a frozen dessert, which you can make by simply popping your frozen fizzy drink cubes in a food processor and serving immediately.

BREWED DRINKS

	🌡*	F.F.	❑	🍭
Coffee, black (for making cold drinks)	✓	✓	✓	✓
Tea, black (for making cold drinks)	✓	✓	✓	✓

ALCOHOLIC DRINKS

	F.F.	⬡	🍦**
Cocktails*	✓	✓	✓
Prosecco/sparkling wine	✓	✓	✓
Red wine	✓	✓	✓
White wine	✓	✓	✓

*As much as I'd *love* to make this a reference guide of different freezable cocktails, I'm keeping it general for the sake of my liver! What I want you to know is that if you're having a party and want to serve cocktails, you should definitely experiment with prepping them in advance. If you'll be serving the cocktail straight from the freezer, remember to add the equivalent amount of water before freezing as you would usually add ice. Depending on the amount of alcohol in your cocktail, it's unlikely that it'll freeze solid, but if it does you can pop it in some cold water to thaw, or break it up and blitz in a blender.

**Please note that, if you want to make lollies, you'll need to add other ingredients to your booze otherwise they won't freeze solid..

OTHER DRINKS

	F.F.	⬡	🍦
Coconut water (2 months)	✓	✓	✓
Protein shake	✓	✓	✓
Smoothies*	✓	✓	✓

*In case you're wondering, it's fine for you to use frozen fruit to make a smoothie and then freeze the smoothie, as long as you do it quickly and as long as the fruit is suitable to use without cooking (see pages 255–61).

Fruits

All fruits can be frozen, they just need a thorough wash and dry first. It's usually better to chop or separate them into smaller pieces where possible, so they can be more easily used straight from frozen. It is important that the fruits are ripe *before* you freeze them so they taste as good as possible from the freezer.

You can freeze fruits with their skin, but if you're likely to use the fruit peeled, it's best to peel them before freezing. Freezing citrus fruits whole actually makes zesting them a lot easier (while they're still frozen), but you'll then need to use the whole fruit.

Although you can defrost fruits in the fridge to eat, many are better used or eaten straight from the freezer. Frozen berries and grapes in particular make a delicious and healthy snack (please don't give whole frozen grapes and berries to kids though; just as when they're fresh, they can be a choking hazard). They're also fabulous in smoothies, sorbets and served with yoghurt, porridge or ice cream.

If you've bought ready-frozen fruits such as berries, always check the packaging to make sure they don't need to be cooked before eating (some may require cooking for safety reasons). If it says they need to be defrosted before using, contact the manufacturer directly to ask if this is for safety or quality reasons – often this isn't actually necessary and the product can be used straight from frozen.

Perfect uses for frozen fruits include:

- Eating frozen in bite-size pieces (allow to soften slightly first!)

- Smoothies

- Ice creams, ice lollies and sorbets

- Crumbles and other fruit puddings

- Savoury cooking

- Sauces and purées

- Baking (look for recipes that use frozen fruits for best results)

- Served frozen with porridge, ice cream or yoghurt

- Cocktails

- Used as ice cubes in drinks

If you're tight on space, you could cook/purée your fruits and store them in usable quantities flat-frozen in freezer bags, but remember they'll then need to be used in one go and won't be suitable for reheating more than once. To provide more flexibility you could freeze the cooked fruits in cubes, but these will be bulkier to store. Alternatively, if you flat-freeze in a very thin layer, you should be able to break a small piece off as and when you need it. If you've got little kids, you can freeze shop-bought fruit purées too (just check with the manufacturer first). These can then be defrosted in the fridge and eaten cold or heated through – just make sure you heat them thoroughly and then cool them down, rather than just warm them (see the advice given on page 106).

TOP TIP

If you're concerned about any fruits (particularly apples and pears) browning while you're prepping them, you can place them in a bowl of cold water and lemon juice (use one tablespoon of lemon juice to one cup of water). I've found that if you work quickly and get them into the freezer, this step isn't always necessary!

BERRIES & GRAPES

	🛁	🔪	O.F.	F.F.	⬡
Blackberries	✓	-	✓	✓ (cooked or puréed)	✓
Blackcurrants	✓	-	✓	✓ (cooked or puréed)	✓
Blueberries	✓	-	✓	✓ (cooked or puréed)	✓
Cranberries	✓	-	✓	✓ (cooked or puréed)	✓
Elderberries	✓	-	✓	✓ (cooked or puréed)	✓
Gooseberries	✓	-	✓	✓ (cooked or puréed)	✓
Grapes	✓	-	✓	✓ (cooked or puréed)	✓
Loganberries	✓	-	✓	✓ (cooked or puréed)	✓
Mulberries	✓	-	✓	✓ (cooked or puréed)	✓
Persimmons	✓	-	✓	✓ (cooked or puréed)	✓
Raspberries	✓	-	✓	✓ (cooked or puréed)	✓
Redcurrants	✓	-	✓	✓ (cooked or puréed)	✓
Sloe berries	✓	-	✓	✓ (cooked or puréed)	✓
Strawberries	✓	✓	✓	✓ (cooked or puréed)	✓

TOP TIP

If you are eating your berries straight from the freezer, they're best eaten within 1–3 months. The longer they are stored, the greater the loss of quality in terms of flavour and appearance.

CITRUS FRUITS

	🧺	〰️	🔪	O.F.	F.F.	⬡
Clementines	✓	✓	✓	✓	✓ (juiced)	✓ (juiced)
Grapefruit	✓	✓	✓	✓	✓ (juiced)	✓ (juiced)
Kumquats	✓	–	✓	✓	✓ (juiced)	✓ (juiced)
Lemons	✓	✓	✓	✓	✓ (juiced)	✓ (juiced)
Limes	✓	✓	✓	✓	✓ (juiced)	✓ (juiced)

CITRUS FRUITS cont.

	🫧	🌀	🔪	O.F.	F.F.	⬡
Mandarins	✓	✓	✓	✓	✓ (juiced)	✓ (juiced)
Oranges	✓	✓	✓	✓	✓ (juiced)	✓ (juiced)
Pomelos	✓	✓	✓	✓	✓ (juiced)	✓ (juiced)
Satsumas	✓	✓	✓	✓	✓ (juiced)	✓ (juiced)
Tangerines	✓	✓	✓	✓	✓ (juiced)	✓ (juiced)

TOP TIP

Citrus fruits can be frozen whole (with peel), in wedges (with peel), in slices (with peel), in segments (without peel), zested or juiced. Frozen slices are particularly lovely as a replacement for ice cubes in drinks. The peel and zest can also be frozen, ready for candying or use in baking.

CORE FRUITS* & FIGS

	⊔	🍐	〰	🔪	🍊	O.F.	F.F.	⬡
Apples (cooking)	✓	✓	✓	✓	✓	✓	✓ (cooked or puréed)	✓ (cooked or puréed)
Apples (eating)	✓	✓	✓	✓	✓	✓	✓ (cooked or puréed)	✓ (cooked or puréed)
Figs	✓	✓	✓	✓	-	✓	✓ (cooked or puréed)	✓ (cooked or puréed)
Pears	✓	✓	✓	✓	✓	✓	✓ (cooked or puréed)	✓ (cooked or puréed)

*Core fruits can be frozen peeled or unpeeled depending on how you plan to use them. I prefer to peel them as the peel can become tough in the freezer. Always remove the core and seeds before freezing.

MELONS

	⊔	🍐	〰	🔪	O.F.	F.F.	⬡
Cantaloupe	✓	✓	✓	✓	✓	✓ (puréed)	✓ (puréed)
Galia	✓	✓	✓	✓	✓	✓ (puréed)	✓ (puréed)

MELONS cont.

	🧺	🥑	〰️	🔪	O.F.	F.F.	📦
Honeydew	✓	✓	✓	✓	✓	✓ (puréed)	✓ (puréed)
Watermelon	✓	✓	✓	✓	✓	✓ (puréed)	✓ (puréed)

STONE FRUITS

	🧺	🥑	〰️	🔪	🍊	O.F.	F.F.	📦
Apricots	✓	✓	-	✓	✓	✓	✓ (puréed)	✓ (puréed)
Avocados	✓	✓	✓	✓	✓	✓	✓ (puréed)	✓ (puréed)
Cherries	✓	✓	-	✓	-	✓	✓ (puréed)	✓ (puréed)
Damsons	✓	✓	✓	✓	-	✓	✓ (puréed)	✓ (puréed)
Dates	✓	✓	-	✓	-	✓	✓ (paste)	✓ (paste)
Greengages	✓	✓	-	✓	-	✓	✓ (puréed)	✓ (puréed)
Lychees	✓	✓	✓	✓	-	✓	✓ (puréed)	✓ (puréed)
Mangoes	✓	✓	✓	✓	-	✓	✓ (puréed)	✓ (puréed)
Nectarines	✓	✓	-	✓	-	✓	✓ (puréed)	✓ (puréed)

STONE FRUITS cont.

	🧺	🥑	🌀	🔪	🍋	O.F.	F.F.	🧊
Olives	✓	✓	-	✓	-	✓	✓ (chopped)	✓ (chopped)
Peaches	✓	✓	-	✓	✓	✓	✓ (puréed)	✓ (puréed)
Plums	✓	✓	-	✓	-	✓	✓ (puréed)	✓ (puréed)

TOP TIP

You don't *have* to cut up small stone fruits, such as olives or cherries, but it can be helpful to do so. If you're going to add olives to a pizza, it's handy to have them cut in half so that they don't roll away! If you don't want to cut them in half, simply use a metal straw to push the stones out.

TROPICAL FRUITS

	🧺	🥑	〰️	🔪	🍊	O.F.	F.F.	❄️
Banana	✓	–	✓	✓	✓	✓	✓ (puréed)	✓ (puréed)
Coconut	✓	–	✓	✓	–	✓	✓ (shredded)	✓ (shredded)
Dragon fruit	✓	–	✓	✓	–	✓	✓ (puréed)	✓ (puréed)
Guava	✓	–	✓	✓	–	✓	✓ (puréed)	✓ (puréed)
Kiwi fruit	✓	–	✓	✓	–	✓	✓ (puréed)	✓ (puréed)
Papaya	✓	✓	✓	✓	–	✓	✓ (puréed)	✓ (puréed)
Passion fruit	✓	–	✓	✓	–	–	✓	✓
Pineapple	✓	✓	✓	✓	–	✓	✓ (puréed)	✓ (puréed)
Pome-granate	✓	–	✓	✓	–	✓	✓ (juiced)	✓ (juiced)
Star fruit	✓	–	–	✓	–	✓	✓ (puréed)	✓ (puréed)

Vegetables

In the tables that follow, I've split the veg listed into those that I recommend blanching (see page 78 for how to do this) and those that I never bother to blanch (as well as a handful that need cooking fully). For those I recommend blanching, you can totally test out freezing them without blanching. However, I've included the blanching timings in both tables in case your preference is to blanch everything (which is a good idea if you're going to be storing your veg for more than a few months).

When it comes to prepping, the most important thing is to cut your veg in a way that works for you (chunks, sliced, diced etc) depending on how you most often use them. You may wish to store the same vegetable prepped in a variety of ways (such as carrot slices, grated carrot and carrot batons) for different purposes. Chucking an unprepped vegetable in the freezer whole is rarely going to be helpful to anyone.

For most people, the ideal approach is to peel and cut up your veg and open-freeze it. But I have also included flat-freezing and cube-freezing in the tables below as you could, of course, purée them if you're tight on space and planning to make soup. Or you might be in the process of baby weaning. If you decide not to blanch your veg, just make sure you always wash it thoroughly.

VEGETABLES I BLANCH

	🫕	🔪	🍋	⌇⌇⌇ 🍲	O.F.	F.F.	⬦
Artichokes, globe (whole)	✓	✓	✓	7–9 mins	✓	✓ (cooked & puréed)	✓ (cooked & puréed)
Artichokes, globe (hearts)	✓	✓	✓	5 mins	✓	✓ (cooked & puréed)	✓ (cooked & puréed)
Artichokes, Jerusalem	✓	✓	✓	3–5 mins	✓	✓ (cooked & puréed)	✓ (cooked & puréed)
Asparagus	✓	✓	-	2–4 mins	✓	✓ (cooked & puréed)	✓ (cooked & puréed)
Aubergine	✓	✓	✓	4 mins	✓	✓ (cooked & puréed)	✓ (cooked & puréed)
Baby corn	✓	✓	-	2–3 mins	✓	-	-
Beansprouts	✓	-	-	3 mins	✓	-	-
Broad beans	✓	-	-	2 mins	✓	✓ (cooked & puréed)	✓ (cooked & puréed)
Broccoli	✓	✓	-	2–4 mins	✓	✓ (cooked & puréed)	✓ (cooked & puréed)
Broccoli, Tenderstem	✓	-	-	3 mins	✓	✓ (cooked & puréed)	✓ (cooked & puréed)

VEGETABLES I BLANCH cont.

	🧺	🔪	🍋	♨	O.F.	F.F.	⬦
Brussels sprouts	✓	✓	-	3–5 mins	✓	✓ (cooked & puréed)	✓ (cooked & puréed)
Butternut squash	✓	✓	-	2 mins	✓	✓ (cooked & puréed)	✓ (cooked & puréed)
Carrots (batons)	✓	✓	-	2–3 mins	✓	✓ (cooked & puréed)	✓ (cooked & puréed)
Carrots (diced)	✓	✓	-	2 mins	✓	✓ (cooked & puréed)	✓ (cooked & puréed)
Carrots (sliced)	✓	✓	-	2 mins	✓	✓ (cooked & puréed)	✓ (cooked & puréed)
Cauliflower	✓	✓	✓	2–3 mins	✓	✓ (cooked & puréed)	✓ (cooked & puréed)
Celeriac	✓	✓	✓	1–2 mins	✓	✓ (cooked & puréed)	✓ (cooked & puréed)
Chicory	✓	✓	-	3–4 mins	✓	✓ (cooked & puréed)	✓ (cooked & puréed)
Corn on the cob	✓	✓	-	4–6 mins	✓	-	-
Edamame beans	✓	-	-	10 secs	✓	✓ (cooked & puréed)	✓ (cooked & puréed)
French beans (green beans)	✓	✓	-	2 mins	✓	✓ (cooked & puréed)	✓ (cooked & puréed)

VEGETABLES I BLANCH cont.

	🧺	🔪	🍋	♨	O.F.	F.F.	⬡
Kohlrabi	✓	✓	-	1–3 mins	✓	✓ (cooked & puréed)	✓ (cooked & puréed)
Mangetout	✓	-	-	1 min	✓	-	-
Parsnips	✓	✓	-	2 mins	✓	✓ (cooked & puréed)	✓ (cooked & puréed)
Peas	✓	-	-	1–1½ mins	✓	✓ (cooked & puréed)	✓ (cooked & puréed)
Potatoes (new)	✓	-	-	5 mins	✓	-	-
Potatoes (chips/ wedges)	✓	✓	-	2 mins	✓	-	-
Potatoes (roast)	✓	✓	-	4–6 mins	✓	-	-
Pumpkin	✓	✓	-	2 mins	✓	✓ (cooked & puréed)	✓ (cooked & puréed)
Purple sprouting broccoli	✓	-	-	2–4 mins	✓	✓ (cooked & puréed)	✓ (cooked & puréed)
Radishes (summer)	✓	✓	-	1–1½ mins	✓	-	-
Radishes (winter)	✓	✓	-	2 mins	✓	-	-

VEGETABLES I BLANCH cont.

	🧺	🔪	🍋	♨	O.F.	F.F.	🧊
Rhubarb	✓	✓	-	1 min	✓	✓ (cooked & puréed)	-
Runner beans	✓	✓	-	2–3 mins	✓	✓ (cooked & puréed)	✓ (cooked & puréed)
Salsify	✓	✓	-	2 mins	✓	✓ (cooked & puréed)	✓ (cooked & puréed)
Sugar snap peas	✓	-	-	1–1½ mins	✓	-	-
Sweet potato (wedges)	✓	✓	-	3–5 mins	✓	✓ (cooked & puréed)	✓ (cooked & puréed)
Spring greens	✓	✓	-	1–3 mins	✓	✓ (cooked & puréed)	✓ (cooked & puréed)
Swede	✓	✓	-	2 mins	✓	✓ (cooked & puréed)	✓ (cooked & puréed)
Swiss chard	✓	✓	-	2 mins (stalks) 1 min (leaves)	✓	✓ (cooked & puréed)	✓ (cooked & puréed)
Turnips	✓	✓	-	2 mins	✓	✓ (cooked & puréed)	✓ (cooked & puréed)

Now, you may think I'm mad for including lettuce, cucumber and other salad items in this table. Of course, you cannot freeze them and defrost them to use in a salad, but you can add your lettuce to smoothies, stir fries or soups. Your frozen cucumber is great instead of ice in your drinks (or in smoothies). And your peppers, onions and tomatoes can all be used straight from frozen in cooked dishes such as lasagne.

VEGETABLES I DON'T BLANCH (BUT SOME CAN BE)

	🧺	🔪	♨	O.F.	F.F.	⬡
Cabbage, Chinese	✓	✓	1–1½ mins	✓	✓ (cooked & puréed)	✓ (cooked & puréed)
Cabbage, red and white	✓	✓	1–1½ mins	✓	✓ (cooked & puréed)	✓ (cooked & puréed)
Cabbage, spring	✓	✓	1–1½ mins	✓	✓ (cooked & puréed)	✓ (cooked & puréed)
Carrots (grated)	✓	grated	-	✓	-	-
Carrots (tops)	✓	✓	-	✓	-	-
Cauliflower (riced)	✓	grated	-	✓	-	-
Celery	✓	✓	3 mins	✓	✓ (cooked & puréed)	✓ (cooked & puréed)
Courgettes	✓	✓	2–3 mins	✓	✓ (cooked & puréed)	✓ (cooked & puréed)

VEGETABLES I DON'T BLANCH (BUT SOME CAN BE) cont.

	🛁	🔪	♨️	O.F.	F.F.	⬡
Cucumbers	✓	✓	-	✓	✓ (cooked & puréed)	✓ (cooked & puréed)
Fennel	✓	✓	3 mins (sliced) 5 mins (quartered)	✓	✓ (cooked & puréed)	✓ (cooked & puréed)
Leeks	✓	✓	2–3 mins	✓	✓ (cooked & puréed)	✓ (cooked & puréed)
Lettuce	✓	✓	2 mins	✓	✓ (cooked & puréed)	✓ (cooked & puréed)
Kale	✓	✓	2 mins	✓	✓ (cooked & puréed)	✓ (cooked & puréed)
Marrow	✓	✓	2–3 mins	✓	✓ (cooked & puréed)	✓ (cooked & puréed)
Mushrooms	wiped clean	✓	Can be sautéed	✓	✓ (cooked & puréed)	✓ (cooked & puréed)
Mustard greens	✓	✓	2 mins	✓	-	-
Okra	✓	✓	3–4 mins	✓	✓ (cooked & puréed)	✓ (cooked & puréed)
Onions, brown & red	✓	✓	1–2 mins	✓	-	-
Pak choi	✓	✓	2 mins	✓	✓ (cooked & puréed)	✓ (cooked & puréed)

VEGETABLES I DON'T BLANCH (BUT SOME CAN BE) cont.

	⊔	⚔	♨	O.F.	F.F.	⬡
Peppers (bell or capsicum)	✓	✓	2–3 mins	✓	✓ (cooked & puréed)	✓ (cooked & puréed)
Rocket	✓	-	1 Min	✓	-	-
Shallots	✓	✓	1–2 mins	✓	-	-
Spinach	✓	-	1–2 mins	✓	✓ (cooked & puréed)	✓ (cooked & puréed)
Spring onions	✓	✓	-	✓	-	-
Stir-fry veggies (ready-prepared pack)	✓	-	-	✓	-	-
Tomatoes, cherry	✓	✓	-	✓	-	-
Tomatoes, other*	✓	✓	-	✓	-	-

*Tomato skins can become tough when frozen, then as you use them in cooking, they end up floating in your sauces. They're perfectly edible, but some people aren't keen on them, so you may wish to peel your tomatoes before freezing. To peel them, simply pour boiling water over your frozen tomatoes, allow to sit for a moment and then drain. You should then be able to carefully slip the skins off (be careful though as they will be hot).

VEGETABLES I FULLY COOK

	🛁	🔪	♨ 🍲	🌡*	O.F.	F.F.	⬡
Beetroot	✓	✓	25–50 mins	✓	✓	-	-
Potatoes (jacket/baked)	✓	-	45–60 mins (bake)	✓	✓	-	-
Potatoes (mashed)*	✓	✓	15 mins	✓	-	✓	✓
Sweet Potato (mashed)*	✓	✓	10 mins	✓	-	✓	✓

*Adding some butter and cheese to your mash can help to bind it when freezing. When reheating, don't be put off by the excess water released. Reheat from frozen in a pan or the microwave, stirring often until this has evaporated.

Herbs, Garlic & Aromatics

If you have ever bought herbs from the supermarket and they've wilted within hours of entering your home, this is going to blow your mind. No more wasting herbs for you, because you can freeze them all!

Woody herbs can be washed, dried and frozen whole in freezer bags or, if you prefer, you can strip the herbs from the woody stems before freezing so they are ready to sprinkle into whatever you are cooking.

Although you can freeze soft herbs in the same way, they won't be suitable to use as a garnish or in a salad after freezing. You can freeze the herbs as a whole bunch or chop up the leaves ready to use in your cooking. There's no need to open-freeze them, simply pop the herbs in a freezer bag after washing and drying (a salad spinner is a useful tool here!).

If you have a lot of herbs, a great suggestion from one member of The Full Freezer Family (my free Facebook group) is to wash and dry them, then squeeze them together into a tight bundle and tie with string, if you prefer, then store in a freezer bag. You can then quickly slice off exactly what you need, when you need it, and return your herb bundle straight to the freezer!

Both woody and soft herbs can be frozen into cubes,

either in softened butter, olive oil or water. Once the cubes are solid, pop them into labelled freezer bags and you're good to go!

There's no need to defrost any herbs before using them, simply chuck them straight into whatever you're cooking – unless you want some herby butter with your steak, in which case you may want to let it thaw in the fridge overnight.

It's worth pointing out that you can also buy frozen herbs from most major supermarkets these days, so if you want to save yourself a job, you can pop whatever herbs you want onto your next shop.

When it comes to your garlic and aromatics, they can be popped straight into a freezer bag to be chopped, grated or minced later, straight from frozen. In fact, ginger and chillies are far easier to grate when frozen. Alternatively, if you'd rather prep them before freezing you can do this and freeze in cubes, then store in a freezer bag once solid.

WOODY HERBS

	⊔	🔪	⬦	▭
Bay leaves	✓	✓	✓	✓
Curry leaves	✓	-	-	✓

WOODY HERBS cont.

	🧺	🔪	⬦	📄
Lime leaves	✓	-	-	✓
Lemongrass	✓	-	-	✓
Marjoram	✓	✓	✓	✓
Oregano	✓	✓	✓	✓
Rosemary	✓	✓	✓	✓
Sage	✓	✓	✓	✓
Thyme	✓	✓	✓	✓

SOFT HERBS

	🧺	🔪	⬦	📄
Basil	✓	✓	✓	✓
Chives	✓	✓	✓	✓
Coriander	✓	✓	✓	✓
Dill	✓	✓	✓	✓
Mint	✓	✓	✓	✓
Curly parsley	✓	✓	✓	✓

SOFT HERBS cont.

	🧺	🔪	🧊	📄
Flat leaf parsley	✓	✓	✓	✓
Tarragon	✓	✓	✓	✓
Thai basil	✓	✓	✓	✓
Watercress	✓	-	✓	✓

GARLIC, CHILLIES & OTHER AROMATICS

	🧺	🔪	🧊	📄
Chillies, bird's-eye	✓	✓	✓ (grated or chopped)	✓
Chillies	✓	✓	✓ (grated or chopped)	✓
Garlic	wiped clean	✓	✓ (puréed or chopped)	✓
Garlic, wild	✓	✓	✓ (puréed or chopped)	✓
Ghost peppers	✓	✓	✓ (grated or chopped)	✓
Habanero chillies	✓	✓	✓ (grated or chopped)	✓
Horseradish	✓	✓	✓ (grated)	✓
Jalapeño peppers	✓	✓	✓ (grated or chopped)	✓

GARLIC, CHILLIES & OTHER AROMATICS cont.

	🧺	🔪	⬡	▭
Lemongrass (2 months)	✓	✓	✓ (grated or chopped)	✓
Root ginger	✓	✓	✓ (grated or chopped)	✓
Saffron	✓	✓	✓	✓
Stem ginger	✓	✓	✓ (with syrup & water)	✓
Truffles	wiped clean	-	✓ (grated)	✓
Turmeric	✓	✓	✓ (grated or chopped)	✓

TOP TIP

If you want to prep your garlic, ginger or other aromatics in advance, but you don't want a whole ice cube-sized portion, try open-freezing them in small coin-sized portions on a lined tray instead – once frozen, store them wrapped in foil in a freezer bag.

Leftovers

There are three things to consider when freezing any leftovers of cooked or prepared foods (which also apply if you want to batch cook too).

Firstly, have you followed all recommended food safety rules such as cooling the food quickly? You can remind yourself of these guidelines on pages 101–8.

Secondly, where does the food sit in The Full Freezer Loop (page 17)? We know we can refreeze something that has been cooked using raw frozen ingredients, but the key here is 'raw'. Were any of the ingredients in your dish already cooked? For example, have you used leftover cooked chicken in your pasta dish? If so, you'll have already reheated them when you cooked the dish and any leftovers must sadly be disposed of.

Finally, how well will the leftovers freeze and reheat? Now, you might be unsure about this one, but really all you need to consider is the texture of the food and whether cooking it further would be likely to make it mushy, tough or generally unpleasant. It's never worth taking up freezer space with something that won't get eaten.

It's worth bearing in mind that if the food can be frozen, defrosted and eaten cold (such as a cheesecake) then it'll most likely be fine. If you do find it goes mushy, next time try it while it's still slightly frozen.

The most important thing is to portion up your leftovers *before* freezing, so you can then take only what you need from the freezer. By doing this, your food will be faster to defrost and reheat, plus you won't have leftovers of your leftovers which can't be refrozen.

As with other sections in this guide, I've included some ideas for freezable dishes on the following pages, but these lists are not exhaustive – just because something isn't there, it doesn't necessarily mean it can't be frozen.

You'll notice in the tables on pages 278–84 that I have said you can flat-freeze dishes that would normally be frozen in a block (for example, lasagne). While you can't freeze the constructed dish, you can freeze the component parts, which I find takes up far less space and means you can get your dish on the table with very little planning. Doing this gives you flexibility around what you cook as you can use component parts in a number of ways (e.g. a bolognese which could be used with spaghetti or to make a lasagne).

And if you're stocking up your freezer for feeding a little one, remember you can just take whatever's left over from your dinner and freeze it in small portions for easy meals. These could be flat-frozen (see page 72) in small freezer bags or cube-frozen (see page 75).

SAVOURY DISHES*

	🌡*	🔪	O.F.	F.F.	🍱	📄
Arancini	✓	-	✓	-	-	✓
Beef stroganoff	✓	-	-	✓	-	-
Biryani (2 months)	✓	-	-	✓	-	-
Bolognese	✓	-	-	✓	-	-
Bone broth	✓	-	-	✓	-	-
Bourguignon (beef or mushroom)	✓	-	-	✓	-	-
Braised cabbage	✓	-	-	✓	-	-
Breaded chicken (e.g. nuggets, escalopes, schnitzel)	✓	-	✓	-	-	-
Calzone	✓	-	✓	-	-	✓
Cannelloni	✓	✓	-	✓	✓	-
Casserole	✓	-	-	✓	-	-
Cassoulet	✓	-	-	✓	-	-
Cauliflower cheese	✓	-	-	-	✓	-
Cheese straws	✓	-	✓	-	-	-
Chicken Kyiv	✓	-	✓	-	-	✓

SAVOURY DISHES cont.

	🌡*	🔪	O.F.	F.F.	🍱	📜
Chilli con carne	✓	-	-	✓	-	-
Chip-shop chips (freshly cooked)	✓	-	✓	-	-	-
Chow mein	✓	-	-	✓	-	-
Coq au vin	✓	-	-	✓	-	-
Corn chowder	✓	-	-	✓	-	-
Cottage pie	✓	-	-	✓	✓	-
Courgette fritters (2 months)	✓	-	✓	-	-	✓
Curry, meat	✓	-	-	✓	-	-
Curry, chickpea	✓	-	-	✓	-	-
Dahl	✓	-	-	✓	-	-
Egg muffins	✓	-	✓	-	-	✓
Empanadas	✓	-	✓	-	-	✓
Enchiladas	✓	-	-	✓	✓	-
Fajita filling	✓	-	-	✓	-	-
Falafels	✓	-	✓	-	-	✓
Fish pie	✓	-	-	✓	✓	-

SAVOURY DISHES cont.

	🌡*	🔪	O.F.	F.F.	🍱	📄
Fish cakes (uncooked)	✓	-	✓	-	-	✓
Frittata	✓	✓	✓	-	-	✓
Goat's cheese tart	✓	✓	✓	-	-	✓
Goulash	✓	-	-	✓	-	-
Gratin dishes	✓	-	✓	-	✓	-
Halloumi fries	✓	-	✓	-	-	-
Jambalaya	✓	-	-	✓	-	-
Jerk chicken	✓	-	✓	-	-	-
Kebabs (2 months)	✓	-	✓	-	-	-
Kedgeree (without boiled egg)	✓	-	-	✓	-	-
Koftas	✓	-	✓	-	-	✓
Lancashire hotpot	✓	-	-	✓	-	-
Lasagne	✓	-	-	✓	✓	-
Macaroni cheese	✓	-	-	✓	✓	-
Meatloaf	✓	✓	✓	-	-	-
Moussaka	✓	-	-	-	✓	-

SAVOURY DISHES cont.

	🌡*	🔪	O.F.	F.F.	🍱	📄
Nut roast (2 months)	✓	✓	✓	-	-	✓
Onion bhajis (1 month)	✓	-	✓	-	-	✓
Pakoras (1 month)	✓	-	✓	-	-	✓
Pasta bake	✓	-	-	-	✓	-
Pies (with pastry top)	✓	✓	✓	✓	✓	-
Pinwheels	✓	-	✓	-	-	✓
Pizza (uncooked) (2 months)	✓	-	✓	-	-	-
Potato cakes	✓	-	✓	-	-	✓
Pulled pork	✓	-	-	✓	-	-
Quiche	✓	✓	✓	-	-	✓
Ratatouille	✓	-	-	✓	-	-
Rice pilaf	✓	-	-	✓	-	-
Risotto	✓	-	-	✓	-	-
Sandwiches (1 month)	✓	✓	✓		-	✓
Sausage rolls (freshly cooked)	✓	-	✓	-	-	✓

SAVOURY DISHES cont.

	🌡*	🔪	O.F.	F.F.	🧊	📄
Shepherd's pie	✓	-	-	✓	✓	
Soups	✓	-	-	✓	-	-
Spanokopita (2 months)	✓	✓	✓	-	-	✓
Stews	✓	-	-	✓	-	-
Stock	✓	-	-	✓	-	-
Stuffing (2 months)	✓	✓	✓	-	-	-
Tartiflette (1 month)	✓	✓	✓	-	-	✓
Teriyaki chicken	✓	-	-	✓	-	-
Toad in the hole	✓	-	-	-	✓	-
Vegetables (cooked)**	✓	✓	✓	-	-	-

*Here I've focused on freezing cooked leftovers to avoid waste, but if you're batch cooking you might prefer to freeze some of these foods before cooking.
**Cooked vegetables won't freeze and reheat particularly well as they're likely to end up overcooked, but they can absolutely be used in other dishes such as fried rice or soup.

SWEET DISHES

	🌡*	🔪	O.F.	F.F.	🫙	🍱	📦
Baked Alaska (1 month)	✓	✓	✓	-	-	✓	✓
Cheesecake (baked) (2 months)	✓	✓	✓	-	-	-	✓
Cheesecake (no bake) (2 months)	-	✓	✓	-	-	-	✓
Cobbler	✓	✓	✓	✓	-	✓	✓
Crumble, fruit (or just the crumble topping)	✓	✓	✓	✓	-	✓	✓
Energy bites	-	-	✓	-	-	-	-
Fudge	✓	-	✓	-	-	-	✓
Granola bars (2 months)	✓	-	✓	-	-	-	✓
Icing, buttercream	-	-	-	✓	-	-	-
Icing, cream cheese (frosting)	-	-	-	✓	-	-	-
Icing, glacé	-	-	-	✓	-	-	-
Jam tarts	✓	-	✓	-	-	-	✓
Meringue	✓	-	✓	-	-	-	-
Mousse (sweet) (2 months)	-	-	-	-	✓	-	-
Overnight oats	-	-	-	✓	✓	-	-
Pies, fruit	✓	✓	✓	-	-	✓	✓
Pie, lemon meringue	✓	✓	✓	-	-	-	✓

SWEET DISHES cont.

	🌡️*	🔪	O.F.	F.F.	🫙	🍱	▭
Pies, mince	✓	-	✓	-	-	-	✓
Pie, Mississippi mud	✓	✓	✓	-	-	-	✓
Pie, pecan	✓	✓	✓	-	-	-	✓
Porridge	✓	-	-	✓	✓	-	-
Pudding, bread and butter	✓	✓	✓	-	-	✓	✓
Pudding, chia (1 month)	✓	-	-	✓	✓	-	-
Pudding, Christmas	✓	✓	✓	-	-	✓	✓
Pudding, rice	✓	-	-	✓	✓	-	-
Pudding, steamed sponge	✓	✓	✓	-	-	✓	✓
Pudding, sticky toffee	✓	✓	✓	-	-	✓	✓
Tart, Bakewell	✓	✓	✓	-	-	-	✓
Tart, fruit	✓	✓	✓	-	-	-	✓
Tarte Tatin (2 weeks)	✓	✓	✓	-	-	-	✓
Tiramisu	-	✓	✓	-	-	✓	✓

*If you're a fan of entertaining, you might be wondering if you can prep any of these desserts in advance to defrost and serve at your next gathering. In some cases, this works a treat, but the best thing you can do is find a recipe that specifies it's suitable. Search online for 'prep-ahead' and 'freezer-friendly' puddings to find something tried and tested that won't disappoint when you dish it up. Remember, if doing this you won't be able to freeze any leftovers, so make sure everyone's got room for pudding!

Pantry
(Tinned, Jarred or Dry Goods)

This is absolutely my favourite category of food to freeze. That's largely because these are the foods that always used to go back in the cupboard or into the fridge, never to be seen again, but also because they're the foods that seem to surprise people the most!

Nuts, Seeds & Dried Fruits

Although we think of nuts as being pretty shelf-stable, oxygen, light and heat can actually cause the unsaturated fats in them to go rancid fairly quickly. Pine nuts, for example, only stay fresh for a month or two at room temperature. Storing them in the freezer helps get around this. For me, the best part is being able to just grab a handful to finish off a meal. I toast them straight from frozen or allow them to come to room temperature before crushing and sprinkling on puddings.

You can freeze the nuts in or out of their shells, and if you always use them chopped, flaked or crushed, you can totally do this before freezing. You can also toast or roast nuts before freezing, but they'll last longer if you freeze them whole.

Seeds and dried fruits tend to have a much longer shelf life than nuts, but keeping them in the freezer is still a great way to avoid any going to waste, especially if it's something you don't use very often. The texture can change as a result of freezing though, so if you want them for snacking, you may want to eat them still frozen (just mind your teeth!). If you're not keen on them as a snack after freezing then use them in cooked dishes.

As with all foods, wrapping your nuts and seeds in some extra foil will help to better preserve them for longer. You should be cautious of keeping them near anything strong smelling, such as onions, as they can absorb these flavours. There's no need to open-freeze them, I've never had an issue with nuts or seeds clumping together!

NUTS*

	🔪	▭
Almonds	✓	✓
Brazil Nuts	✓	✓
Cashews	✓	✓
Chestnuts	✓	✓
Hazelnuts	✓	✓

NUTS cont.

Macadamias	✓	✓
Peanuts	✓	✓
Pecans	✓	✓
Pine nuts	-	✓
Pistachios	✓	✓
Walnuts	✓	✓

*If you toast the nuts before freezing, be sure to cool them to room temperature before wrapping and putting in the freezer.

SEEDS

Chia seeds	✓
Flaxseed (ground)	✓
Flaxseed (whole)	✓
Pumpkin seeds	✓
Sesame seeds	✓
Sunflower seeds	✓

DRIED FRUITS

	🔪	▭
Dried blueberries	-	✓
Dried cherries	-	✓
Dried cranberries	-	✓
Dried stoned dates	✓	✓
Dried goji berries	-	✓
Dried mango	-	✓
Dried mixed fruits	-	✓
Dried pineapple	-	✓
Dried soft apricots	-	✓
Dried soft figs	-	✓
Dried soft prunes	-	✓
Dried strawberries	-	✓
Glacé cherries	-	✓
Mixed peel	-	✓
Raisins	-	✓
Sultanas	-	✓

Flour & Yeast

I know you probably think I've lost the plot, but freezing your flour is actually a great habit to get into. Little bugs called weevils can live in flour and freezing them actually helps to kill off their eggs and prevents infestations. Nothing special needs to be done, just transfer your flour to a freezer bag and chuck it in the freezer. The cold won't freeze it solid, just chill it, so it won't need defrosting as such, just let it come up to room temperature before use. If desired, you could double bag the flour to avoid it picking up any smells from other foods, and to better protect it.

FLOUR & YEAST*

Bread flour	-	-
Buckwheat flour (2 months)	-	-
Coconut flour	-	-
Plain flour	-	-
Self-raising flour	-	-
Yeast (fresh)	✓	✓
Yeast (dried)	-	-

*There's no need to chop or wrap flour or dried yeast, simply put them straight into a freezer bag before putting them into the freezer.

Beans & Pulses

If you use half a tin of beans or pulses (or if you've bulk
cooked some dried ones), the leftovers can be drained
and frozen. If desired, you could freeze in a tub in usable
portions in the water they came in, but this will fill up far
more freezer space and will take much longer to thaw.
For ultimate convenience, I rinse and drain any tinned
beans or pulses, pat dry and open-freeze before placing
in a freezer bag. This way you can just use a handful as
needed and throw them straight into whatever you're
cooking.

BEANS & PULSES

	❄	🌡*	O.F.
Black beans (tinned or home prepped)	✓	✓	✓
Butter beans (tinned or home prepped)	✓	✓	✓
Cannellini beans (tinned or home prepped)	✓	✓	✓
Chickpeas (tinned or home prepped)	✓	✓	✓
Kidney beans (tinned or home prepped)	✓	✓	✓
Lentils (tinned or home prepped)	✓	✓	✓

Grains & Sides

Obviously, there's no need to start freezing dried cupboard staples, but if you happen to cook more than you need, it is possible to freeze the leftovers as long as they are cooled quickly (see page 101 for more on why this matters). This is particularly handy if you're guilty of always cooking too much rice or pasta.

Ideally rice and pasta should be undercooked slightly so they don't end up overcooking when you reheat them, but don't let that put you off giving freezing a go. If you're concerned that your rice or pasta will end up overcooked, use them in dishes like arancini or a pasta bake where it won't matter as much.

If you're flat-freezing, be sure to either freeze in individual portions or in a thin layer inside the bag so you can just break off as much as you want to cook. If you're eating your grains cold then be sure to defrost them in the fridge, but if you're heating them, you can do so without defrosting. Simply blast in the microwave in short bursts, stirring to ensure the heat is evenly distributed, or heat on the hob in whatever sauce you may be using until piping hot throughout.

Gnocchi is the only food listed in the following table as best frozen uncooked; this is because it cooks so quickly and will become mushy on the outside before it's fully heated through. If you have made your own gnocchi or have a pack that contains more than you can eat, freeze it before cooking and when ready to eat, it can be cooked through straight from frozen.

GRAINS & SIDES*

	🌡*	O.F.	F.F.	⬡
Bulgur wheat (cooked)	✓	-	✓	✓
Couscous (cooked)	✓	-	✓	✓
Gnocchi (uncooked)	✓	✓	-	-
Noodles, egg (cooked)	✓	✓	-	-
Noodles, udon (cooked)	✓	✓	-	-
Orzo (cooked)	✓	-	✓	✓
Pasta (cooked)	✓	✓	-	-
Pearl barley (cooked)	✓	-	✓	✓
Polenta (cooked)	✓	-	✓	✓
Quinoa (cooked)	✓	-	✓	✓
Rice, white and brown (cooked)	✓	-	✓	✓

*Rice and pasta contain the bacteria Bacillus cereus which can make you very ill. Cool these quickly (within an hour) using the advice on page 101 and make sure they are defrosted safely and reheated thoroughly (page 106) when you're ready to eat them.

Tinned & Jarred Food

If you only need to use part of a tin of meat or fish, freezing is a good way to avoid it ending up in the bin (just check with the manufacturer that this is safe to to do). Remove from the tin, drain off any liquid or jelly and pat it dry with some kitchen paper before portioning it into usable quantities. It will be prone to freezer burn, so don't freeze for more than 2 months, and wrap tightly to help protect it.

For tinned fruit and vegetables, drain and open freeze these so you can just use as much as you need. Any 'wet' products (such as coconut milk) can be flat-frozen or frozen in cubes. Just remember some foods may not freeze solid (e.g. mincemeat) so test a small amount first if you're unsure.

TINNED MEAT & FISH

	🔥	🔪	O.F.	F.F.	📄
Chopped pork (2 months)	✓	✓	✓	-	✓
Corned beef (2 months)	✓	✓	✓	-	✓
Danish ham (2 months)	✓	✓	✓	-	✓
Spam (chopped pork and ham) (2 months)	✓	✓	✓	-	✓
Tinned chicken (2 months)	✓	✓	✓	-	✓

TINNED MEAT & FISH cont.

	🍳	🔪	O.F.	F.F.	📖
Tinned mackerel (2 months)	✓	-	-	✓	✓
Tinned salmon (2 months)	✓	-	-	✓	✓
Tinned sardines (2 months)	✓	-	✓	-	✓
Tinned tuna (2 months)	✓	-	-	✓	✓

TINNED FRUIT & VEG

	🍳	O.F.	F.F.
Tinned apricots	✓	✓	✓ (juice)
Tinned broad beans	✓	✓	-
Tinned carrots	✓	✓	-
Tinned green beans	✓	✓	-
Tinned hearts of palm	✓	✓	-
Tinned jackfruit	✓	✓	-
Tinned mushrooms	✓	✓	-
Tinned peaches	✓	✓	✓ (juice)
Tinned peas	✓	✓	-
Tinned pineapple	✓	✓	✓ (juice)

TINNED FRUIT & VEG cont.

		O.F.	F.F.
Tinned potatoes	✓	✓	-
Tinned sweetcorn	✓	✓	-
Tinned tomatoes	-	-	✓
Tomato passata	-	-	✓

OTHER TINNED & JARRED FOODS

	F.F.		
Aquafaba (chickpea water)	✓	✓	-
Baked beans*	✓	✓	-
Coconut cream	✓	✓	-
Coconut milk	✓	✓	-
Coconut oil	-	✓	-
Condensed milk	-	-	✓
Evaporated milk	✓	✓	-
Mincemeat	✓	-	✓
Spaghetti hoops*	✓	✓	-

*If you have some leftover tinned baked beans or spaghetti hoops, these can be frozen prior to reheating. Their consistency can be affected when thawed and reheated though, so you may want to use these in other dishes such as chilli or in pasta recipes.

Sweets & Snacks

I can't say that we ever have chocolate that's at risk of going to waste, but I have found hiding it in the freezer to make it last longer is pretty effective! I've no doubt professional chocolatiers will be massively contesting this one, and I agree it is worth exercising some caution if you have a box of particularly posh chocolates, but chocolate can indeed be frozen.

To keep it at its best quality and minimise the risk of white 'bloom' (where the fats or sugars in the chocolate have risen to the surface), it's best to move the chocolate to the fridge before freezing and defrost it in the fridge before moving to room temperature. I'll be honest though, as long as it's not so hard it'll break my teeth, I just eat it straight from the freezer with a hot coffee. Occasionally, I keep a stash of dark chocolate in the freezer to add straight to my chilli for extra depth of flavour.

On the savoury side of things, items such as crisps, popcorn and tortilla chips can be frozen, but they're best eaten straight from the freezer. If you're putting them in a lunchbox, it's a good idea to decant them into a smaller bag. If they are left out in the air, they can turn stale quite quickly. I encourage you to try them straight out of the freezer though – there's something delightful about a chilled crisp (to accompany a G&T)!

Apart from the chocolate (which it's a good idea to wrap), no special treatment is needed for the items below. Just pop them straight into labelled freezer bags or air-tight tubs (to avoid anything getting crushed).

SWEETS & SNACKS*

Chocolate	✓
Crisps	–
Lentil crisps	–
Marshmallows	–
Popcorn (popped)	–
Prawn crackers	–
Rice cakes	–
Tortilla chips	–
Veggie straw crisps	–

*Be sure to check out page 222 (baked goods) and page 276 (leftovers) for more sweet treats that you can freeze.

What *Can't* I Freeze?

I'm not sure you really need this section. As you know all too well by now, I encourage you to have a crack at freezing any food (as long as it fits within the food safety rules around freezing, defrosting and reheating).

There are some foods that don't freeze particularly well and are difficult to save, however, so I figured it's worth giving you a snapshot! This doesn't mean you can't freeze them within dishes or have a go at freezing them if they'll otherwise go to waste. Just don't end up storing anything in your freezer for the sake of it if you know you're unlikely to use it after freezing. And, if you can, test a small quantity before committing freezer space to larger amounts.

This isn't a comprehensive list, but here are some of the foods I have found do not freeze well:

• **Hard-boiled Eggs** Cooked eggs can be frozen, but the whites of hard-boiled eggs tend to turn very rubbery after freezing and thawing, so they're better cooked fresh. If you do have more boiled eggs than you can eat, though, you can remove the whites and just freeze the yolks to later crumble over salads or add to sandwiches.

- **Creamy Dips or Dishes** Generally speaking, any dips or dishes that are creamy in consistency are likely to split and become grainy after freezing. If they're heading to the bin, you could test out freezing a small quantity, but unless it's something that could be saved by putting it in a sandwich, it's unlikely to be invitingly edible after freezing.

- **Emulsion Sauces** Sauces such as mayonnaise and hollandaise have a tendency to split and are very difficult to save. You can use a small amount of mayonnaise in your frozen sandwiches though if you're not keen on butter.

- **Jelly** If you want to eat jelly as you normally would, the freezer is *not* the place to store it. It will become cloudy and once defrosted it turns mushy. If you freeze it in single-quantity portions (such as in a lolly-mould), it isn't half bad when eaten still frozen though!

- **Salad** As I have flagged in the vegetables section, you can freeze the component parts of a salad (yep, even lettuce and cucumber – see page 268) but freezing them as a ready-made salad to eat later will end in disappointment. If defrosted, salad leaves will become limp and your salad veg will turn soggy. The only way to create a salad using your Freezer Stash is to roast up some frozen veggies and add them to fresh salad leaves.

- **(Most) Takeaway Leftovers** If your takeaway was cooked using raw ingredients then it's fine to freeze any leftovers, but many takeaway restaurants will pre-make at least some elements of your meal in order to deliver it to you faster. This means when they're cooking it for you, they're reheating the food (and we know this shouldn't be done more than once). Some dishes may even have been cooked twice intentionally such as egg-fried rice (a high-risk food!). Whenever we're thinking about freezing a food that has been prepared outside of our own homes, it is important to consider the fact that we don't know how long our food has sat out for, or how safely it was cooked. So when it comes to take away leftovers, you're usually safest to avoid freezing.

ACKNOWLEDGEMENTS

Words cannot express how grateful I am to have been given the opportunity to write this book. Thank you so much to everyone who has helped to make it happen.

To my literary agent, Kate, for plucking me from obscurity, believing in me and helping me to craft my message.

To my editor, Celia, and all of the team at Ebury Press who have made the book what it is. Your support and advice have been invaluable.

To Dem, Francesca and Lara at Ebury Press for helping me to share this book with the world.

To Georgie and Louise for making freezing so pretty. Who knew that was possible?

To Gregg and Chris for your kind words and support, I still can't believe you even know who I am.

To my friends for putting up with my incessant freezer talk, and to those that I have connected with through Instagram over the last few years. When I started on this journey, I had no idea it would lead me to so many wonderful and creative people.

And to all of my family.

Mum, thank you for every conversation, every Facebook post, every summer of childcare and gate crashing your house.

Dad, thank you for being my biggest champion and for proving that The Full Freezer Method is perfect for those who don't cook!

Mike and Rose, for the business chats, and Lin and Nicola, for helping with the kids whenever I was on a deadline.

Ellie and Josh, thank you for being patient on the days when Mummy couldn't play. I hope this book will inspire you to know that you can forge your own path and achieve whatever you put your mind to.

And finally, to Matt. Thank you for always believing in me. For not questioning what I was trying to build, instead trusting that I would create something of value. I couldn't have done this without you.

INDEX